TITANS OF '72

TITANS OF '72
TEAM CANADA'S SUMMIT SERIES HEROES

MIKE LEONETTI
WITH PHOTOGRAPHS BY HAROLD BARKLEY
FOREWORD BY ROY MACGREGOR

DUNDURN
TORONTO

Project Editor: Michael Carroll
Editor: Nigel Heseltine
Design: Jennifer Scott
Printer: Trigraphik LBF

Library and Archives Canada Cataloguing in Publication

Leonetti, Mike, 1958-
    Titans of '72 : Team Canada's summit series heroes / Mike Leonetti ; foreword by Roy MacGregor ; photographs by Harold Barkley.

Issued also in electronic formats.
ISBN 978-1-4597-0766-5

1. Hockey players--Canada--Biography. 2. Canada-U.S.S.R. Hockey Series, 1972. I. Barkley, Harold II. Title.

GV848.5.A1L468 2012   796.962092'271   C2012-903208-5

1   2   3   4   5   16   15   14   13   12

We acknowledge the support of the **Canada Council for the Arts** and the **Ontario Arts Council** for our publishing program. We also acknowledge the financial support of the **Government of Canada** through the **Canada Book Fund** and **Livres Canada Books**, and the **Government of Ontario** through the **Ontario Book Publishing Tax Credit** and the **Ontario Media Development Corporation**.

All interior photographs in this book are by Harold Barkley unless credited otherwise.

Care has been taken to trace the ownership of copyright material used in this book. The author and the publisher welcome any information enabling them to rectify any references or credits in subsequent editions.

J. Kirk Howard, President

Printed and bound in Canada.

Visit us at
Dundurn.com
Definingcanada.ca
@dundurnpress
Facebook.com/dundurnpress

Dundurn
3 Church Street, Suite 500
Toronto, Ontario, Canada
M5E 1M2

Gazelle Book Services Limited
White Cross Mills
High Town, Lancaster, England
LA1 4XS

Dundurn
2250 Military Road
Tonawanda, NY
U.S.A. 14150

This book is dedicated to all the players and coaches
who were part of Team Canada in 1972.

CONTENTS

FOREWORD

We know exactly when countries are founded, but it is an entirely different story when they find themselves. And that is why September 28, 1972, is such a pivotal date in Canadian history. It is not the date of birth, not a mark of victory in war or of any signing of a constitution but a date that holds our mirror to the rest of the world.

A time for our JFK, our Churchill.

If this sounds overreaching, let me explain. If you speak to Americans (and most Canadians) of a certain age, they will know precisely where they stood, what they were doing, perhaps even what they were wearing on November 22, 1963, the day President Kennedy was assassinated in Dallas.

The same applies to Canadians on September 28, 1972.

The British of an earlier generation had their moment in history when the words of a single man, Winston Churchill, spoke for the nation. The prime minister stood in the Parliament of the United Kingdom on June 4, 1940, and told his people: "We shall not flag or fail. We shall go on to the end. We shall fight in France, we shall fight on the seas and oceans, we shall fight with growing confidence and growing strength in the air. We shall defend our island, whatever the cost may be. We shall fight on the beaches, we shall fight on the landing grounds, we shall fight in the fields and in the streets, we shall fight in the hills. We shall never surrender ..."

Many would think it preposterous to connect such pivotal world historical moments to a meaningless exhibition series of a game then played almost exclusively in the north by Canadians, Swedes, Finns, and Russians, but no Canadian hockey fan who lived and died through that long September four decades ago would have a problem with such a stretch.

I can tell you exactly where I was when Paul Henderson scored the goal that turned this extraordinary eight-game series in Canada's favour. Less than three weeks earlier I had married Ellen and was now on my very first real job: working in the editorial pool for Maclean-Hunter business publications. A small magazine dedicated to boats and marine services had tapped me to head up to Lake Simcoe for a promotional piece on a local marina. Having no car, I took the bus. I wore a blue shirt and tie, dark pants. Paul Henderson scored while I waited for a ride down a country road to the marina, me standing with a half-dozen other frozen-in-action Canadians in a small country general store with a small black-and-white television propped up on the counter, the game coming in from the nearby Barrie station on rabbit ears. I was merely one of millions watching the most viewed television program in Canadian history.

Our moon walk, if you will.

By this point, Canadians had largely regained the faith they had lost in their own country only a short time earlier. The 1972 Summit Series was never supposed to be a challenge. It was, rather, to be a demonstration to the world that Canadians not only invented hockey, they ruled hockey. For the first time ever, the best Canadian hockey players — the best in the world, obviously — would play the upstart Soviet Union, a country that hadn't even played the game until the 1950s and had some (smug Canadians thought meaningless) success in the international arena against other countries and some Canadians who simply weren't good enough for the National Hockey League, then completely dominated by Canadian stars.

It would be a sweep, most commentators believed. The Russians would be lucky to win a single game. They had no goaltending. So what if Bobby Orr was hurt. So what if Bobby Hull couldn't play because he had jumped to the World Hockey Association. So what if Jean Beliveau and Gordie Howe had retired. There were still more than enough Canadian superstars to take the series in a walk, let alone a skate.

Canadians had laughed at the Soviets' equipment, laughed at their silly concepts of style of play, laughed when Canada shot ahead 2–0 in the opening moments of the very first game of the eight-game series, with four games to be played in Canada, four more back in Moscow.

That laughter had died away quickly. The Russians — afraid to take slap shots lest they break their sticks, dropping pucks laterally as if they were on a soccer pitch, skating and passing cross-ice as much or more as up and down, all wearing *helmets*, for heaven's sake — tied the game and went ahead to win. By the time the series reached Vancouver for Game 4, Canadian fans, embarrassed and angry and outraged, were booing their heroes loudly as they slinked off the ice following yet another loss to these upstarts.

And this is when Phil Esposito made the speech that, hard as some academic minds find to accept, is surely the most famous speech known in Canadian history.

"To the people across Canada," Esposito said, near-tear eyes turned full on the camera rather than interviewer Johnny Esaw, "we tried, we gave it our best, and to the people that boo us, geez, I'm really — all of us guys are really disheartened and we're disillusioned and we're disappointed…. We cannot believe the bad press we've got, the booing we've gotten in our own buildings. I'm completely disappointed…. I cannot believe it…. Every one of us guys, 35 guys that came out and played for Team Canada, we did it because we love our country and not for any other reason…. We came because we love Canada."

They say this single talk — not heard by a single other player, incidentally — was the turning point. Not so much in the team, perhaps, but in the fans. Ashamed, they turned to belief. Belief became inspiration in Moscow — the Canadian flag waving, the Canadian players defiant, at times to the point of foolishness, little-known players suddenly taking on the heroic cloth it had always been expected others would wear.

And then one other voice that stands as familiar as the plaintive plea of Esposito. This time it was Foster Hewitt in triumph: "Here's another shot! Right in front! They score! Henderson has scored for Canada! Henderson right in front of the net and the fans and the team are going wild! Henderson right in front of the Soviet goal with 34 seconds left in the game!"

Our defining moment.

And all captured here again in the evocative words of Mike Leonetti and the brilliant photography of the late Harold Barkley.

Titans of '72 is not a sports book. It is, rather, one country's history.

ROY MACGREGOR
Ottawa
June 2012

ACKNOWLEDGEMENTS

I would like to thank all those at Dundurn Press for their assistance in getting this book completed. Special thanks to Michael Carroll, Dundurn's associate publisher and editorial director, for allowing me to do *Titans of '72*.

INTRODUCTION
Titans of '72 Gave Canada the Series of the Century

By the time the calendar turned to September 28, 1972, the Canada-Russia series was up for grabs since the two teams had battled to a 3–3–1 record in the first seven games. The date of the final game was firmly etched in the minds of every Canadian who was alive in 1972, but everyone would tell you it wasn't supposed to happen this way. Team Canada, most believed, was going to roll over its Russian counterpart and win all the games or at least have an easy time of it. Those sentiments went with the eight-game series that had words like *friendly, exhibition, learning, cultural exchange,* and *sportsmanship* tossed around when the series was first announced in April 1972. By the end of September, all those politically correct words were long ejected from the vocabulary and words such as *war, exhaustion, must win, backs to the wall,* and *life and death* had replaced them. Sure, it was still a hockey series, but it had become so much more than that as the month of September unfolded.

Both Canada and Russia wanted the 1972 hockey series between the two countries to happen, but for different reasons. Canada wanted to show that the Russians weren't going to win every major hockey competition by rolling over what was now perceived as inferior Canadian teams. The best professionals from Canada (which meant National Hockey League players) would put the Soviets in their place, and they weren't going to be subtle about it. The Canadians who negotiated the deal that set the series up for the month of September 1972 insisted that Canada not be restricted in any way in whom they could play in this competition. The Russians had always resisted this notion, saying that the Canadian players had to be "amateurs" just like theirs, even though everyone knew the Russian players were well-trained professionals themselves. This time the Soviets relented and agreed to the new terms because they wanted Canada back in international tournaments. The Russians were winning far too easily most of the time (at the Olympics or at the World Hockey Championships), so they welcomed the idea of going up against superior players. The Russians were also anxious to show that the communist system wasn't nearly as bad as the Western world believed. An eight-game series against Canada would give them a small chance to show their way of life was something to be admired as well. There was no trophy (like the Stanley Cup) or great prize for winning this series but the bragging rights to being called the best hockey country in the world were on the line whether it was outwardly stated or not.

As much as the communist country wanted to show its human side, the Canadian players were just as intent on showing that their system — hockey or political — was indeed the better one. Hockey fans watching in Canada may not have grasped the political warfare between communism and democracy, but the players surely believed there was more at stake than just a series of hockey games. It was "us" versus "them" all the way from Montreal to Moscow but there was little to choose from on the ice. Part of the problem between the players was that they could not communicate with each other, which may not have been a bad thing at the time but some barriers might have fallen if they could all speak English or Russian. The only time the two teams appeared friendly to each other was during the exchange of gifts prior to the start of each game. Smiles and handshakes were part of the routine before the puck dropped but certainly not afterward! The Canadians were all about emotion whereas the Soviets rarely displayed any emotion — good or bad — and this only added to the differences between the two teams.

Even though the NHL wasn't directly involved in the discussion to set up the 1972 series, it was the league's willingness to allow the series to use its players that made it all possible. NHL President Clarence Campbell got the owners on side with the proviso that all the players selected were from NHL teams only. The executive director of the National Hockey League Players' Association was Alan Eagleson, and he assured that the players would participate provided their pension fund was enhanced with some of the proceeds of the series. NHL stars were essentially told they were playing, and there wasn't much choice for most of them. Vacation plans were altered, the last half of summer was given up, and other commitments were cancelled because their country was calling on them (a few players managed to wriggle out for a variety of reasons). So there was no way to say no to Eagleson's strong-arm tactics. In addition to heading the NHLPA, Eagleson also doubled as a player agent, which meant many on Team Canada's roster were his clients.

This eight-game series between Canada and Russia would hopefully set up future international hockey gatherings where more nations would be involved (like the Canada Cup, the World Cup, and NHLers playing in the World Championships, and later, the Winter Olympic Games), but that was for the future. Right now it was Canada versus the Soviet Union for eight games — four in Canada and four in Moscow — one time only, and it has never been repeated in a similar way.

When the Canadian players reported to training camp on August 13, 1972, few thought the series was going to be anything too difficult. After all, who had the Russians beaten that were as good as the team Canada was going to put together in September 1972? They were told by advance scouts that the Soviet goaltending was weak and that the Russians weren't going to handle the physical play of the Canadian club. Even if they had been told differently there was no way any Canadian player was going to believe anything until he had a reason to do so. Practically all the experts picked Team Canada to romp to victory and some suggested that anything but eight straight wins would be a disappointment. A few voices warned that the Soviets were much stronger, but their protestations seemed to be unheard and unwanted. Team Canada should have consulted more closely with those who had more recent experience in international hockey, but there was a firm belief this group of all-stars would simply overwhelm the Russians.

It was easy to understand why Team Canada was so highly favoured. They were strong in net with Montreal's Ken Dryden and Chicago's Tony Esposito, both award-winning netminders. The defence was anchored by New York's Brad Park (the best NHL blueliner after Bobby Orr) and Montreal's Serge Savard, a Conn Smythe Trophy winner. Guy Lapointe was another Montreal rearguard who had won a Stanley Cup already, while Pat Stapleton and Bill White were the best two players on the Chicago Black Hawks blueline. Tough, hard-edged veteran defencemen on the roster included Don Awrey, Gary Bergman, and Rod Seiling.

Brad Park (left) and Gary Bergman jostle with the Soviets. (Hockey Hall of Fame)

The most impressive part of Team Canada's roster was the firepower of forwards Phil Esposito, Yvan Cournoyer, Frank Mahovlich, Peter Mahovlich, and Paul Henderson. Other sharpshooters included Mickey Redmond, Dennis Hull, Bill Goldsworthy, and Rod Gilbert. Good playmakers featured Stan Mikita, Jean Ratelle, Bobby Clarke, and Red Berenson, while size, strength, and checking would fall on the shoulders of Ron Ellis, Jean-Paul Parise, Wayne Cashman, and Vic Hadfield, who could all score, as well! If coach Harry Sinden wanted to inject some youth into the lineup, he could call upon Gilbert Perreault, Marcel Dionne, Dale Tallon, and a few others. In short, Canada had a skilled roster with the ability to play the game in a variety of ways, but they had never played together as a team prior to their training camp.

Peter Mahovlich scores on Soviet goalie Vladislav Tretiak in Game 2 in Toronto. (Hockey Hall of Fame)

Canada's lineup was missing two very significant players both named Bobby — Hull and Orr. Hull was banned from playing in the series because he had signed with the new professional league, as were a few others (such as Derek Sanderson, J.C. Tremblay, and Gerry Cheevers — all high-quality hockey players). There was a national reaction to Hull's exclusion to the team but the NHL was adamant that he wasn't going to play if he wasn't under contract to a league club. Orr's surgically repaired knee wasn't ready to let him play. Orr was on the Team Canada roster but it was clear by the time the team headed over to Sweden that the best player in hockey wasn't available for any of the games. The presence of both superstars would have helped Team Canada immensely, but the club wasn't too worried since they had more than enough NHL stars to fill the void.

However, the Russians with the funny-sounding names who nobody in Canada knew anything about prior to the series could also play the game. They also had the benefit of playing together in competition previously, and that would make a big difference early in the series. Vladislav Tretiak was a stand-up goalie who played his angles very well. The Soviets had some good size on defence with the likes of Alexander Gusev, Gennady Tsygankov, and Victor Kuzkin (the Russian team captain) able to patrol effectively on the blueline. Yuri Liapkin and Vladimir Lutchenko provided some attack from the Soviet defensive group.

Just like the Canadian squad, the Russians had many skilled and talented forwards who could all skate and put the puck in the net. Alexander Yakushev was their best all-round forward while Valery Kharlamov could dance on his skates and would cause all sorts of trouble for Team Canada. Vladimir Shadrin, Vladimir Petrov, and Alexander Maltsev all had good size and were always dangerous on the attack. The Russians had two gritty agitators in Boris Mikhailov and Yevgeny Mishakov and they drew the ire of more than one of the Team Canada players. As talented as these players were, none had ever played against the best of the NHL and were expected to cower once they got on the ice with the formidable team of all-stars. The superbly conditioned Soviets never let that happen and were often the better team especially in Canada where they only lost one game of four.

One of those trying to capture the attention of the Canadian players was head coach Sinden who had some international experience as a player in the late 1950s. Sinden had never played in the NHL but he was a good junior and senior player who understood the Russians were not coming in to this series expecting to be wiped out. Assistant coach John Ferguson, a recently retired NHL player, was chosen to help keep the players in line and to aid in getting Sinden's points across. He also listened to player beefs and there were plenty as the series started. But the Canadian players were not really listening and there were too many of them — 35 — to worry about, more than a pair of coaches could deal with effectively. After three weeks of training and playing intra-squad games the group that became known as Team Canada thought they were ready for the night of September 2, 1972, in Montreal — the date and location of the opening game.

The Canadian side was so high for this game that they could not wait for the opening face-off. Phil Esposito represented Canada for the ceremonial face-off when Canadian Prime Minister Pierre Trudeau dropped the puck. Kuzkin represented the Soviets as team captain but he had no chance to win this draw. Esposito snapped the puck back as if he was protecting a late-game lead in his own end, and then had to chase the puck down so he could give it to Trudeau! The intensity of Team Canada was obvious and then they scored 30 seconds into the game. Another goal before the game was seven minutes old made it 2–0, and it looked as if the rout was on and this was only the first game!

However, some of the Canadian players quickly realized the Russians were going to be formidable opponents. Henderson and Cournoyer understood the Soviets were physically stronger than anticipated and in great condition — much better than Team Canada at that moment. The Russians tied the game and then got ahead 4–2 before weathering a brief Canadian comeback in the third period to win 7–3. Suddenly everyone associated with Team Canada had explaining to do and there were few answers available. The Soviets had duped a very arrogant group of Canadian players and waltzed out of the Montreal Forum with the greatest win in Russian hockey history (they had only started to play hockey just after the Second World War).

Sinden now had the attention of all his players and he had to strategize quickly to adapt to the new reality. Canadian wingers had to muck it up along the boards and use their sticks, which meant they had to whack at a Russian attacker and hope the referee wouldn't call a penalty. Team Canada concluded its players needed to slow the Russians down and try to get them to play an NHL style of game. It was downright ugly at times, but the Soviet pattern of circling, which featured short, quick passes to moving targets, had to be disrupted. The precise and well-timed Russian approach to the game had to be upset in some fashion, and there was no time to figure something else out by the second game of the series.

The Canadians became aggressive and took advantage of the American referees (assigned to do the games in Canada) who didn't desire to have the Canadian players or fans on their backs. They let quite a lot go and certain players (Cashman, Goldsworthy, Parise, and Bergman were some of the more notable aggressors) on Team Canada pushed the rulebook to the limit. It worked well in Toronto when Team Canada rebounded to win 4–1 but not so well in Winnipeg when it ended 4–4 and especially not in Vancouver when the Russians won again with a 5–3 triumph. Team Canada was extremely upset about their lack of success and took out many of their frustrations on the Russian players during the games. It was as if they were mad at the Russians for even showing up, let alone playing so well. As the series moved west, it only got worse for the Canadian superstars.

By the time the fourth game in Vancouver was over everyone in Canada had reached the boiling point. The fans were at first shocked (after the Montreal game), then relieved (after the Toronto contest), and then angry about Team Canada and their ineffectual tactics (in Winnipeg and Vancouver). Respect and admiration went to the Russians while the home side was derided and booed severely. Someone had to speak up for the team and it was one of the appointed alternate captains who took it upon himself. Phil Esposito, named player of the game for Canada after the Vancouver debacle, ripped into the entire country during a television interview. He expressed the team's profound disappointment with how they were being treated in Canada and he said it was clear that the Soviets had a good team. However, Esposito closed with a statement rarely repeated when his Vancouver speech is recalled. As he shook hands with interviewer Johnny Esaw, Esposito said, "Johnny, we're going to get better, I know it." The entire interview may have changed the very complexion of the series for the exasperated Canadian team but their character and courage in the face of long odds was about to be tested like never before.

The transformation from a collection of individuals into a unit didn't come about easily. It began when many Canadian hockey fans started offering their support to the team through letters, telegrams, and postcards. Later, an estimated 3,000 screaming fans invaded Moscow and attended each of the four games with shouts of "Go Canada Go." However, the players were still unsure about how this group was going to come together. Many were bitter rivals in the NHL and it was difficult to put that aside quickly. Most were used to playing alongside their NHL teammates and not with a whole group of stars. But in Sweden, while they played two ugly contests against the Swedish national team, the group of widely divergent NHL stars started to become a team. They adjusted to the larger ice surface and got a taste of some questionable judgements by international referees, which helped them prepare for the four games in Moscow.

Having four players leave the team when they reached the Soviet Union wasn't helpful, but this was a very determined group by now and nothing was going to stop them. Sinden and Ferguson settled the team down on defence (going with six regulars) and that was a bigger factor in getting the squad pointed in the right direction. Sinden not only fixed the defensive pairings he also cut down the number of players who were actually going to play. This meant some players were going to be unhappy but the Canadian coaches settled on four lines, six defencemen, and two goalies for the most part and that did a great deal to bring the team together as one unit. Abandoned and unwanted in Canada, elsewhere in the world, Team Canada pulled together and faced adversity as a group. Slowly but surely the team started to regain the support of Canadian hockey fans, and the entire country was entranced by the series Canadians wanted to win so much. The dressing room was soon shut with only those onboard let into the inner sanctum. It was going to be "an all for one" mentality or else it wasn't going to work in the face of a crisis.

If Team Canada was upset in Stockholm, they were no more content in the historic city of Moscow. First, their steaks were stolen, and then the final indignity — all the Canadian beer somehow disappeared! If that wasn't enough, the players were constantly upset by phone calls

The final period of Team Canada's 4–1 victory in Game 2 winds down in Toronto. [Hockey Hall of Fame]

to their rooms with nobody at the other end of the line. Hockey players are creatures of habit and routine and in the Soviet Union those rituals were broken all the time. The Russians were masters of psychological tricks and would do things like disrupt practice times just to upset the opposition. On at least one occasion Sinden was blocked from the Team Canada dressing room but he simply barrelled past the guards and made it through. This didn't make the Canadian players feel any better about the players on the other side of the ice and the pot boiled for all four games in Moscow.

Even though Team Canada blew a big lead in the fifth game and dropped a 5–4 decision, many of the Canadian players gained a great deal of confidence that they could beat the Russians in their own backyard — only now there was no room for error. One more loss or tie and it was over as far as winning the series was concerned. Nevertheless, players like Esposito and Henderson remained steadfast in their belief that it could be done. A 3–2 win in the sixth contest gave Team Canada renewed life, and it now appeared the Russians were the ones who were unsure what to do. The Soviets were upset about how nasty the Canadians were on the ice but still felt the series was in their favour because of home ice and the officiating. The Russians may have made a mistake by keeping Tretiak in net for every game, because by the time the sixth game was over, the young 20-year-old was looking tired especially on Canada's third goal scored by Henderson.

If there was one big mistake the organizers had made it wasn't including the best referees available to do this series. First, they used a two-man system, something the NHL players had never dealt with at all. Second, the European referees used in the Moscow games had no sense of how the NHL players approached the game in a much more physical manner and often over-looked the subtle and obvious stick fouls the Russians doled out. The referees for the Moscow portion of the series were all European-based or from communist bloc countries and not so inclined to give Team Canada any benefit of the doubt. The officials made the temperature of every Canadian player, coach, and fan rise to unprecedented levels but the fact was they were in charge and Team Canada didn't adjust until it was almost too late. Even Sinden, who knew more about this type of officiating than anyone else associated with Team Canada, had a difficult time getting all the emotions under control. He paced miles behind the Canadian bench during the eight games but somehow managed to corral his team just enough to put Team Canada in position to secure a chance to win the series. It was, however, too close for comfort.

The seventh game was the best of the series and the teams stuck to hockey for the most part. It was a close, titanic struggle with Team Canada getting a late goal from the hot stick of Paul Henderson to get a 4–3 win. It was a great individual effort from the streaking left winger who beat two defencemen and goalie Tretiak to get Canada the win. When Team Canada stuck to playing the game (and stopped trying to run over the Russians) they were every bit the squad they were supposed to be, and this game proved they had the skill level necessary to beat anyone.

September 28 was a beautiful day across Canada and the country shut down for the final game of the series. There was a very strong sense in both Canada and Russia that this game was going to be something special and those who stayed home or turned on a television at work or school were not going to miss this game played on a Thursday afternoon. For those who could not get to a TV, the radio broadcast would have to do (with Bob Cole doing the play-by-play), but it was important to watch or listen to this game. Canadians from coast-to-coast gathered to enjoy the action. By this time, the series had captured the attention of all Canadians like no other event had ever done. The 3,000 fans in Moscow had helped buoy the sagging spirits of Team Canada and they were going to be as loud today as they ever were during their stay in the city. The Canadian fans in Moscow came from all over Canada and rocked the Luzhniki Ice Palace (an antiquated arena that roughly held 11,000 seats), which was part of the Lenin Sports Complex located right in the heart of Moscow.

Game 8 nearly got away from Team Canada early on with bad penalties from officials now determined to call interference infractions. They managed to get out of the first period tied 2–2, but try as they might Team Canada was down 5–3 going into the third period. Being the professionals that they were, the Team Canada players decided to play one more period and see where they stood at the end of the game. The plan was to get one early and they did when Esposito knocked one home early at the 2:27 mark of the third. The Russians never could handle Esposito who was big and strong and impossible to move from the slot. The Russians never had to play against a player who positioned himself the way Esposito did, and they

Phil Esposito converses with his brother, goalie Tony Esposito. (Hockey Hall of Fame)

never found a way to deal with the man who was the most determined player on either team. Esposito also helped set up Cournoyer who tied the game 5–5 at the 12:56 mark of the third period.

At this point Eagleson had to be rescued from the grasp of the Russian police and be plunked down along the Team Canada bench for safekeeping. Eagleson wanted the red light turned on after Cournoyer's goal and when he didn't see it come on in a timely fashion he made a point to bring it to someone's attention. The Russian constabulary, which had a strong presence at each and every game, were in no mood to tolerate the volatile Eagleson and were about to haul him away when Peter Mahovlich stepped in and stopped their hasty exit. The scene may have further unnerved the Russians, but it only served to fire up Team Canada even more. They pressed on the attack but time was running out quickly.

It looked as if the series was going to end in a tie, which might have been a fair result, but then word was sent to Eagleson at the Canadian bench late in the game that the Russians would claim victory based on more goals (two) scored. Perhaps this is why Team Canada kept coming on stronger, while the Soviets were more content to preserve the status quo. Eagleson crudely dismissed the messenger and said the series wasn't over yet. Team Canada became even more determined to win the series.

With less than a minute to go, the puck was behind the Russian net when the Soviet defenceman Vasiliev ringed it around the boards hoping to clear the zone. However, Cournoyer was there inside the blueline (having given up on the idea of going to the bench for a line change) and he trapped the puck. At the same time, Henderson had just replaced Peter Mahovlich and he tried to swipe Cournoyer's attempted pass at the Russian net. Henderson tripped and fell into the boards or as Foster Hewitt said on the television broadcast, "Henderson made a wild stab for it and fell."

The puck was now loose in the Russian end but three Soviet players were in position to take it and get back up the ice, giving them what might be the last chance to score. Then the puck rolled off Vasiliev's stick and lay there for just a second in the face-off circle to the right of Tretiak. The unrelenting Phil Esposito got to it first and whacked a shot right on net. By now, Henderson was back on his feet and right in front of the Soviet goal. He shot the puck quickly but Tretiak made the save. The rebound came right back out to Henderson's forehand and he made no mistake putting it home for the game and series winner. "Henderson has scored for Canada!" cried out Hewitt.

As he scored the goal Henderson had a brief moment of melancholy when he thought of how his late father would have loved to share in this moment, but then he was swarmed by Cournoyer, Esposito, and the rest of Team Canada in a wild celebration with 34 seconds still to play. If Henderson felt some pangs of remorse all of Canada was relieved, delirious, celebratory, and just plain happy that the players with the maple leaf on their jerseys had won it all. Everything else was forgotten and forgiven as Canadians from coast-to-coast let loose with a patriotic fervour never seen before and rarely seen since.

The final score in the game was 6–5, and the series went Canada's way by a 4–3–1 count. It was hardly the way it was supposed to go, but Team Canada had overcome great odds to give the country one glorious September nobody would ever forget. The Titans of '72 showed how great heart, determination, and positive thinking could help anyone overcome tremendous obstacles. Every player on Team Canada wanted to avoid being tagged as a loser in the Series of the Century — it would have been something they would never live down the rest of their lives. The pressure made the Canadian team intense and gave them the motivation to stick together. Team Canada backchecked and blocked shots with a desperate intensity. They scratched and clawed their way back into this series and eventually did just enough to win it.

Stan Mikita crashes toward the Soviet net. (Hockey Hall of Fame)

Many took to the streets to celebrate once the game was over, and the hearts of all Canadians swelled with pride over Team Canada's victory. Three days later a large crowd greeted many of the Team Canada players at Toronto's Nathan Phillips Square on the night of October 1, 1972, despite a strong rain. They sang "O Canada" and heard from Phil Esposito who expressed his delight at seeing so many out on a stormy night to acknowledge their hockey heroes for one last time before the players returned to the grind of the NHL.

The series was over, but it would always be remembered in the hearts and minds of all Canadians who watched Team Canada accomplish something very special over 28 days in September 1972. As Foster Hewitt recapped the Canadian effort so eloquently at the close of the final game, "They fought like tigers!" The Russians had trouble understanding the Canadian drive and fire to win and were rather shocked and silent when the final game was over. The headlines claimed Canada was once again "King of Hockey" but the reality was it was by a single goal with just 34 seconds to play — an uneasy climb back to throne by any standard. In the end, it was the emotion displayed by the Titans of '72 that won the "Series of the Century."

In this book we have tried to capture the essence of what happened in September 1972 that so enthralled an entire nation — from the players and coaches to broadcasters, officials, and hockey fans — who witnessed some of the best hockey ever played in one eight-game series. There is a strong focus in this book on the Canadian players who became heroes to an entire country that watched their every play during those games. Enjoy looking back at a glorious moment in time when the Titans of '72 ruled the hockey world and gave us the "Series of the Century!"

Paul Henderson scores what many still feel is the greatest goal ever scored in hockey: Game 8 in Moscow, a victory with 34 seconds to spare. (Frank Lennon/GetStock.com)

THE
PLAYERS

PHIL ESPOSITO
Career Summary

Phil Esposito was still a developing player for the Chicago Black Hawks at the end of the 1966–67 season. The team had finished on top of the six-team league in that year (the first time they had ever done so), but a poor playoff performance got Chicago management thinking they had to make changes. In short order a deal was put together that saw Chicago send Esposito to the Boston Bruins, which was a terrible deal for the Black Hawks. It was a trade that hurt Chicago immeasurably and helped launch a new era in Boston. The deal stunned Esposito, but he was able to get a fresh start in Beantown and show that he wasn't just an ordinary player. He was no longer in the shadow of superstars like Stan Mikita and Bobby Hull.

Esposito's first full NHL season came in 1964–65, when he scored 23 times and added 32 assists. The Black Hawks made it to the Stanley Cup finals that year only to lose in seven games to the Montreal Canadiens. He raised his goal total to 27 the next season, but this time Chicago was eliminated in the first round of the post-season by Detroit. The 1966–67 campaign saw Esposito's point total rise to 61 (21 goals, 40 assists), as he thrived as the centre on a line with the goal-scoring Hull and defensive-minded winger Chico Maki. The Black Hawks looked as if they were in good position to win the Stanley Cup for the first time since 1961. However, the veteran Toronto Maple Leafs (a club loaded with players over the age of 30) had other ideas and upset the Black Hawks (a team they trailed by 17 points in the regular season) in six games. Esposito had no goals and no assists and admitted that the Leafs had done a good job of shutting him down in the series.

Shortly before being traded to Boston, the outspoken Esposito told Chicago management that they would mess up a good team that could win for years and his prediction turned out to be true. Coach Billy Reay and general manager Tommy Ivan didn't appreciate Esposito speaking his mind and didn't want anything more to do with him or to watch another poor playoff performance. On May 15, 1967, the trade was completed sending the six-foot, one-inch, 210-pound Esposito to Boston, a perennial basement-dwelling team. "I was in shock. I was no longer a Black Hawk. I was a Boston Bruin. You don't think that you're ever going to be traded," Esposito said years later. Hull told Esposito at the time of the deal, "Go to Boston, play good hockey and show these jerks what a mistake they made." Esposito took his former teammate's advice to heart and made the deal one of the greatest and most memorable trades in NHL history.

The Bruins gave up little (Pit Martin, Gilles Marotte, and goalie Jack Norris) to add Esposito, Ken Hodge, and Fred Stanfield to a team rebuilding around arguably the greatest player in hockey history — Bobby Orr. The Bruins started to roll and Esposito not only led the NHL in points in 1968–69 (126), he also helped them to be Cup champions in 1970 and 1972. He became one of the most prolific point producers in NHL history and had six seasons of 100 or more points in Boston. As good as Esposito was in the NHL, his greatest moment came during the 1972 Canada-Russia Series.

Phil Esposito does what he does best: going for the net.
This time the victim is the Toronto Maple Leafs' Johnny Bower.

'72 Series Performance

Able to escape the shadow of Bobby Hull (ruled ineligible) and Bobby Orr (injured) for this series, Phil Esposito played superbly for the entire eight games versus the Soviets. It started in the first game of the series when he scored the opening goal just 30 seconds in and ended when he assisted on Paul Henderson's dramatic winner with 34 seconds to play in the last contest to give Canada a 4–3–1 edge in games.

The final game in Moscow saw Esposito deliver what was one of the greatest performances in hockey history. Esposito scored the opening goal for Canada to tie the game 1–1 and helped his team defensively by going behind goalie Ken Dryden to stop a sure Soviet goal with the Russians already leading in the game 4–3. Down two to start the third period, Esposito scored early to make it 5–4 and then assisted on Yvan Cournoyer's goal to tie the game at 5–5. Esposito refused to leave the ice as the game was coming to a close and was able to whack a loose puck at the Russian goal that Henderson eventually put away to give the Canadians a thrilling come-from-behind victory.

Throughout the series Esposito was the emotional leader of the team, the heart and soul of a squad made up of NHL superstars yet in dire need of someone to take control. Esposito took control and his leadership made him one of the most admired people in all of Canada during a magic month of hockey.

"Looking back, it was one hell of a series," Esposito said years later. "It was the toughest thing I ever had to do in my life as a hockey player. The mental anguish we all went through was overwhelming. And I was never able to play at that level again. From that moment on, for me as a player, it was all downhill."

Phil Esposito was traded to Boston in May 1967.

Esposito was dealt to the New York Rangers in 1975. He helped them reach the Stanley Cup final in 1979. He finished with 717 goals and 1,590 points in 1,282 career games while racking up points, awards (winning the Art Ross Trophy four times and taking the Hart Trophy twice), and championships to become one of the true superstars in the game.

While Team Canada decided not to name an official team captain for the '72 series, Phil Esposito, Frank Mahovlich, Jean Ratelle, and Stan Mikita were all given an "A" on their sweaters for the designation of alternate captain. Of the four players chosen, only Esposito played in all eight games against the Soviets, and in fact became the team leader in every way imaginable.

PAUL HENDERSON
Career Summary

For most hockey fans, Paul Henderson first came into prominence when he was part of the big trade that sent Frank Mahovlich from Toronto to Detroit. Many forget that the speedy Henderson played in the last four seasons of the "Original Six" for the Detroit Red Wings. After a stellar junior career with the Hamilton Red Wings (49 goals in 1962–63), Henderson joined Detroit for 32 games in the 1963–64 season. The Red Wings were defeated by the Maple Leafs in a seven-game Stanley Cup final, but Henderson had performed well (two goals and five points in 14 playoff games) in the post-season. He scored 22 times in 1965–66, a rare feat for a young player in this era, and then managed to record 21 goals in just 46 games during an illness-plagued 1966–67 season. Detroit was anxious to make changes the following year and Toronto coach and general manager Punch Imlach always coveted the five-foot, 11-inch, 180-pound Henderson for the Maple Leafs. The March 3, 1968, deal shocked the hockey world and Henderson was off to Toronto with Norm Ullman and Floyd Smith.

Paul Henderson parks himself in front of Chicago Black Hawks goalie Denis DeJordy.

At first, Henderson was upset by the trade since he had been in the Red wing system for so long but he soon came to appreciate the history that came with the Leafs and playing in Maple Leaf Gardens. He thrived in the hockey environment and loved the fact that he would be on *Hockey Night in Canada* every Saturday. He soon became a consistent 20-plus goal scorer and he eventually found himself on a line with Ullman and Ron Ellis. The line was the Leafs' best unit for a number of years with the fleet-footed, hard-shooting left winger scoring 27, 20, and 30 markers before notching 38 goals in 1971–72, his career-best total. It set him up for an invitation to Team Canada's training camp in September 1972.

'72 Series Performance

When left winger Paul Henderson departed to attend Team Canada's 1972 training camp in Toronto in August, he wasn't at all sure of where he would place on the team. Henderson had to compete with and beat out top-calibre NHL stars like Frank Mahovlich, Yvan Cournoyer, Dennis Hull, Vic Hadfield, and J.P. Parise to gain a spot on left wing. If there was one thing in Henderson's favour, it was that he came to the camp in great physical condition. He was very well prepared for the heat of the early days of the camp, as was Ellis. The Toronto linemates were afraid they were going to be assigned the young diabetic kid from Philadelphia named Bobby Clarke, but that actually turned out quite well for all concerned. They played at a high tempo in training, which gained them the respect of the coaches, and the trio was named to start the series against the Soviets in Montreal. Henderson and Clarke both scored in the opener and that kept their line intact for the next game.

In fact, the line played in all eight games of the history-making series. Clarke and Ellis checked effectively to play a more defensive game while Henderson would score a series-leading seven goals (and 10 points, second only to Phil Esposito's 13). Henderson played the greatest hockey of his life and was a constant concern for the Soviet team. He played best in Moscow over the final four games of the series, with the wider ice surface. He was nearly badly injured in the fifth game of the series (a contest that saw him score two goals), but luckily he was wearing a helmet when he hit the end boards with a thud. He suffered a concussion but insisted he be allowed to play.

By the sixth game of the series, the Canadian squad was forced into a position where it had to win all three remaining games; Henderson would score the winner in each of those contests. His goal to win the seventh game was truly a spectacular individual effort. With the teams playing four-on-four, Henderson took a pass from defenceman Serge Savard but had two Russian defencemen to beat as he crossed the opposition blueline. He beat one defender with a move to the inside but the other rearguard came to take Henderson out with a bodycheck. Somehow, he managed to move the puck forward and got his stick free. Just as he was hitting the ice from the check, Henderson put a rising shot over Vladislav Tretiak for the winning goal. He was mobbed behind the net by his delirious teammates. There was only 2:06 left to play when he scored to make the eighth game relevant.

"Of all the goals I scored I never got that much satisfaction before," Henderson said after the seventh contest. "It's something to have 18 players like the ones on this team congratulating you." Henderson finished his impossible dream when he knocked in his own rebound with 34 seconds to play in the last game of the series to give Canada a 6–5 win.

After the final game was over Henderson stated that it was the biggest thrill of his career to be named to Team Canada and that his second biggest thrill was actually making the squad after camp was over. "And now, three winning goals in a row. Who can believe it? This is the happiest moment of my career," Henderson stated. The last of his three game winners is forever etched in the mind of every Canadian who watched the final contest on that Thursday afternoon in Moscow. Paul Henderson emerged to be the unlikely but never forgotten hero!

Paul Henderson was so confident at the end of the '72 series that he called teammate Peter Mahovlich off the ice with less than one minute to go because he was sure he could score the winning goal. "I let him on because he told me to get off, he was going to score a goal," Mahovlich said. Phil Esposito who assisted on the winning goal said, "I saw Henderson flying in. I fired on the net and the rebound went to Paul and he put it away."

KEN DRYDEN
Career Summary

Just before Ken Dryden turned 17 years of age, he was drafted 14th overall by the Boston Bruins during the NHL's second ever amateur draft held on June 11, 1964. The process was so secretive that the names of all the players chosen weren't publicly released at the time. However, just over two weeks later the Montreal Canadiens made a four-player trade to acquire the rights to the young netminder and then tried to convince Dryden to play junior hockey for the Peterborough Petes. The lanky goalie who valued his education had his own ideas about where he was going to play and instead chose to attend Cornell University in the United States. Dryden's first season at the Ivy League school was the 1966–67 campaign (which ended in a NCAA championship for Cornell) and he would play in 83 career games for his college team, winning 76 times and suffering just four losses!

Dryden still resisted pro hockey for a year with the Canadian National Team in 1969–70 but eventually signed with the Canadiens for the 1970–71 campaign. He was assigned to the Montreal Voyageurs of the American Hockey League for some pro experience. He posted a very impressive 16–7–8 record for the Voyageurs and by March 1971, the Habs were willing to give the six-foot, four-inch, 205-pound Dryden a shot to play in the big league. He won his

Goalie Ken Dryden backstopped the Montreal Canadiens to six Stanley Cups in 1971, 1973, and 1976–79. (Dennis Miles)

first start and went on to record a perfect 6–0 record to finish the regular season. Montreal was to face the Boston Bruins in the first round of the playoffs and nobody expected that Canadiens coach Al MacNeil would chose Dryden as his starter but he did so when Phil Myre and Rogie Vachon faltered late in the year.

Montreal had trouble with the high-scoring Bruins but wouldn't quit and eventually forced a deciding game in Boston, winning it by a 4–2 score. Dryden continually frustrated the Bruins attack, facing a total of 286 shots — from the likes of Phil Esposito, Bobby Orr, Johnny Bucyk, and Ken Hodge who were the top four players in the NHL scoring race during the 1970-71 season. Over the seven-game series, Dryden never flinched and did his best to hold his team in a series where all the odds were stacked against them.

A rather modest Dryden said that pressure wasn't new to him. "Maybe I appear very cool but the pressure is there and I feel it. It's a relative thing, though. I felt it in college and international hockey in the big games. So pressure isn't exactly new to me. I think it took a couple of games for our club to realize how good we really are. In the second game we got behind but we never quit. We came back to win it and that told us we could win the series."

The Canadiens then beat Minnesota in the next round before edging out Chicago in seven games during the Stanley Cup final to complete their unexpected run to the championship. Dryden was named winner of the Conn Smythe Trophy as the MVP of the 1971 playoffs, another honour that helped launch a great career. The Habs were ousted by the New York Rangers in 1972, but Dryden was named the NHL's best rookie and his brief but impressive history made him a surefire candidate to be selected for Team Canada.

'72 Series Performance

Dryden got the call to begin the '72 series in Montreal in front of his NHL fans but it turned out very badly when the Soviets scored almost at will after Canada had started out with a 2–0 lead. The Soviets tied the game before the first period was over and then poured in five more with their 30 shots on goal. Dryden looked helpless on almost all of the Russian goals and his defencemen did little to help him in a very hot and humid Montreal Forum. He wasn't any better in Vancouver three games later and Canada went down to a 5–3 defeat. The Russians only took 30 shots on Dryden, but the star netminder still found himself fishing the puck out of his net after yet another great passing play by the Soviets.

Tony Esposito started the first game in Moscow and had a good outing until the third period of the contest. Team Canada blew a 4–1 lead and the 5–4 loss had Canada on the brink of losing the series. Coach Harry Sinden went to Dryden for the sixth game and he turned in a solid performance, making 27 saves and giving up just two goals. It seemed as if Dryden was going to play the rest of the series but Esposito got another chance in the seventh game. However, Sinden liked that Dryden had played and succeeded in pressure-packed NHL games and gave him the start for the final and deciding contest.

The final game in Moscow was hard on the goalies, as a 6–5 score might indicate, but Dryden had absolutely no chance on the Soviet goals. He did make 22 saves and then sprinted down the ice like no other goalie has ever done to help congratulate Paul Henderson on the winning goal and then realized there were 34 seconds to go and scrambled back to his net! Luckily, Canada hung on and the series was finally over with Team Canada emotionally and physically spent. In the dressing room afterward Dryden observed, "I just looked around the room [and] everyone's uniform was soaked with sweat. I felt really proud for all of us. We had gone from the heights to the depths and now we were back on top again."

In the '72 series, Dryden proved he could still deliver in the clutch and he went on to win five more Stanley Cups with Montreal before deciding to retire at the age of 31. He was elected to the Hall of Fame in 1983.

On December 31, 1975, the Montreal Canadiens with Ken Dryden in goal tied the Russian Central Red Army team 3–3 during a tour of the NHL by Soviet teams. Montreal dominated the game played at the Montreal Forum, but the Russians knocked three past Dryden on only 13 shots. Peter Mahovlich (one assist), Yvan Cournoyer (one goal), Serge Savard (one assist), Guy Lapointe, and Don Awrey, who were Dryden's teammates on Team Canada in '72, also played in the New Year's Eve contest. Eleven of the Russians who played in the Summit Series played in the game against Montreal three years later.

ROD GILBERT
Career Summary

The New York Rangers were looking forward to having Rod Gilbert join their team after he had enjoyed a stellar junior career. They had discovered the five-foot, nine-inch, 180-pound right winger in his native province of Quebec, one of the very few French Canadians to leave the province without joining the Montreal Canadiens (Gilbert's favourite team while growing up). He was assigned to play junior hockey in Guelph, Ontario, and was part of a Memorial Cup–winning team in 1960. He led the OHA in scoring with 103 points the next season. But in his last junior game of the season, Gilbert skated over some debris fans had thrown on the ice. He lost control and crashed heavily into the end boards. Gilbert couldn't feel his legs and was told later in hospital that he had suffered a broken vertebra in his back. The terrified youngster had to face a spinal fusion procedure where a bone from his leg would be moved to his back to tie vertebra together.

After some bad days where he worried every minute about the status of his injury, Gilbert's leg began to recover, as did the rest of his body. He was back playing in the 1961–62 season (after missing about half a season), and got into some minor league games before he was called up to the Rangers for the playoffs. He acquitted himself very well while taking a regular turn on the ice, and scored his first ever NHL goal on April 3, 1962, against Johnny Bower of Toronto in the semi-final series between the Maple Leafs and the Rangers. The Rangers didn't win the playoff series versus Toronto, but Gilbert now had the confidence he could play in the big league.

Gilbert scored 11 times in his first full season but then had 24- and 25-goal seasons to establish himself as an NHL sniper. However, partway through the 1965–66 season, Gilbert had to go back and have another operation because the graft completed previously had loosened too much. He nearly died just after the second operation, but a doctor was able to restart his heart. He once again had to go through a rehabilitation process, but came back to the Rangers at the start of the next season, scoring 28 goals in just 64 games in 1966–67. The 1967–68 season saw Gilbert make good use of his strong shot to connect for 29 goals and his best night came on February 24, 1968, in his hometown of Montreal when he took 16 shots on goal and scored four times in one game against the mighty Habs.

Rod Gilbert fends off the Montreal Canadiens' Jacques Laperriere.

Gilbert had a 30-goal season in 1970–71 but had his best year the following season when he scored 43 times in 1971–72. He was also very good in the '72 playoffs when the Rangers finally broke through to make it to the Stanley Cup finals for the first time since 1950. Gilbert had a four-point game (one goal, three assists) as the Rangers eliminated the Chicago Black Hawks on the night of April 23, 1972, in the second round of the playoffs with a four-game sweep. The Rangers all believed they could win the Stanley Cup, but Boston, led by Bobby Orr, proved to be too much to beat in the finals. The series marked the only time Gilbert (who had seven points in six games versus Boston) played in the finals. As one of the best players on one of the top teams in the NHL for 1972, Gilbert received an invitation to Team Canada for the Summit Series.

'72 Series Performance

Rod Gilbert was in the starting lineup for Team Canada along with his New York Ranger teammates Jean Ratelle and Vic Hadfield. The line didn't have a good outing in Montreal and generated little offence, although they were hardly the only Canadian players to look slow and out of condition after the 7–3 loss. All three were pulled from the lineup and Gilbert didn't reappear until the fourth game of the series in Vancouver.

While Hadfield had difficulty getting back on track, Gilbert and Ratelle started to find their game once they got some practice time in Sweden and Moscow. Gilbert picked up an assist on a goal by J.P. Parise in the fifth game and then added another helper on a goal by Dennis Hull in the sixth contest — a game Canada won 3–2 in a do-or-die situation. Gilbert was performing with an attitude he rarely showed in the NHL and soon earned the nickname "Mad Dog." Growing in confidence now that his role on the team was secure, Gilbert scored a very important goal in the seventh game that gave Canada a 3–2 lead early in the third. He dug the puck out of the corner before backhanding a shot past a surprised Vladislav Tretiak. Canada won that game 4–3 and that set up the final game as a winner-take-all contest.

It was in the eighth game that Gilbert got into a fight (the only brawl of the entire series) with Evgeni Mishakov of the Russian team and although it was more of a wrestling match, the Canadian winger didn't lose the scrap and landed the only

Rod Gilbert in his 18-season career with the New York Rangers scored 406 goals and 615 assists for 1,021 regular season points.

solid punch of the dust-up. In addition to his fight Gilbert set up defenceman Bill White with a beautiful pass to tie the game 3–3 in the middle of the second period — a very important marker at the time. Canada went on to win the game making Gilbert's gritty contribution all the more vital to the cause.

Gilbert's efforts for Team Canada weren't as well remembered as some others, but in the end he had a very important hand in the victory, showing that he wasn't just a skilled player but a very determined one as well.

Rod Gilbert was the first player in the history of the New York Rangers to have his sweater number retired. Number 7 was raised to the rafters of Madison Square Garden to honour his Ranger career that saw him score a team record 406 goals. Other Team Canada players to have their sweater number retired include Ken Dryden, Yvan Cournoyer, Serge Savard, Phil Esposito, Bobby Orr, Rick Martin, Gilbert Perreault, Stan Mikita, Tony Esposito, Bill Goldsworthy, Marcel Dionne, and Bobby Clarke.

BOBBY CLARKE
Career Summary

Bobby Clarke was such a determined young man that he wasn't going to let a disease that might restrict many affect his life much if at all. When Clarke was 14 years old, he was told he had juvenile diabetes. This potentially devastating news could have made life miserable for a young boy who only thought about being a hockey player. He had no fear for his life but he was extremely concerned about his hockey career. Clarke had no interest in school and his father, Cliff, was concerned that his son would end up in the mines like he had. Quitting school at a young age didn't seem like a good idea, but Clarke wanted to dedicate himself totally to hockey. After all the tests were done and the appropriate medication was decided upon, Clarke knew there was no looking back. Doctors told him he could continue playing hockey, which he likely would have done anyway. Diabetes wasn't going to hold him back.

When he turned 17 years of age, Clarke tried out for the Junior A team in Flin Flon. His coach, Patty Ginnell, noted that Clarke wasn't very big — in fact he was quite thin and he wore glasses. However, as soon as Clarke showed what he could do on the ice, Ginnell's worries disappeared. Clarke would lead the Western Hockey League in points for two consecutive seasons (168 in 1967–68 and 186 in 1968–69), and scored 102 goals over that same time span. It was thought that Clarke would be a high pick in the 1969 Amateur Draft but most NHL teams were scared away by the diabetes concerns. Philadelphia scout Gerry Melnyk, however, was a believer in Clarke's abilities and insisted the Flyers take him. Melnyk staked his reputation on Clarke becoming an NHL player and that convinced General Manager Bud Poile that he should select the rugged centre in the second round (although a doctor was consulted before Clarke's name was announced by the Philadelphia club). It wasn't a selection the Flyers would regret.

Many believed Clarke would have to go to the minors to begin his pro career, but he made the Flyers on the first try, with 15 goals and 46 points as a rookie. His goal total swelled over his next four seasons, as he notched 27, 35, 37, and 35 markers, respectively. Clarke oozed leadership and his style on ice was infectious. He was constantly in motion and it seemed that his sheer will would always rule the day for the Flyers. He was soon named team captain of a squad that liked to play the game very physically and would follow their leader with no questions asked. Clarke had filled out to five feet, 10 inches and 185 pounds, but he left the toughness to a group of players whose sole purpose seemed to be to protect their choirboy-faced leader. Good goaltending, great defence, intimidation, and timely goals were the strong points of the Flyers teams of the 1970s.

Even though he had 81 points in 1971–72 and won the Masterton Trophy, the selection of Clarke for Team Canada was something of a surprise, but then the coaches wanted to add some youthful enthusiasm to the team and they got plenty of that from Clarke.

Philadelphia Flyer Bobby Clarke mixes it up in front of the Toronto Maple Leafs' net.

'72 Series Performance

Bobby Clarke was the very first player to show up at Maple Leaf Gardens on August 13, 1972, for the start of Team Canada's training camp. It was also Clarke's 23rd birthday and he was ready to earn a spot on the roster. He told a friend that Canada would win every game by at least three goals! Placed between Toronto wingers Ron Ellis and Paul Henderson, the line was so good in training camp that they earned a spot in the lineup for the entire eight games versus the Soviets. Clarke played the series the exact same way he did in the NHL with his stick doing much of his talking.

Clarke scored in the opening game in Montreal and then again in the first game in Moscow (and added four assists), but he was most effective in the face-off circle where he won many draws for the Canadian squad. Otherwise, he was very good at hounding the Soviet players all over the ice and was naturally involved in the most controversial play of the series. It was suggested to Clarke by assistant coach John Ferguson that he take the lumber to Valeri Kharlamov who was doing more damage to Team Canada than any other Russian player. Clarke didn't have to be told twice and hunted down the slick Russian winger in the sixth game with a vicious two-hand slash across the ankle. Clarke was penalized for his action (during a very close game Canada had to win), but Kharlamov was clearly hobbled. The Russian sniper missed the seventh contest and wasn't as effective in the final game of the series.

Clarke was never really remorseful about his unsportsmanlike play (18 penalty minutes during the series, a total that included a 10-minute misconduct), but years later did suggest he crossed the line with his stick work on Kharlamov. Clarke also termed his stick assault on the Russian star as "necessary" while admitting he wouldn't do such a thing in an NHL game.

Having gained confidence, he was among the best players in the NHL after the Summit Series. The 1972–73 NHL season saw Clarke record 104 points. The Philadelphia Flyers started to become a force in the NHL, and by 1974, the club had made it to the Stanley Cup finals. The Flyers won the championship in six games over the Boston Bruins led by Bobby Orr and Phil Esposito. The tireless Clarke had shown the hockey world that nothing was impossible and that any obstacle could be overcome if you really wanted it bad enough.

Over the course of his NHL career, Bobby Clarke was named the winner of the Hart Trophy on two occasions. He recorded 358 goals and 1,210 points in 1,144 career games. He was elected to the Hockey Hall of Fame, as were 15 others associated with Team Canada in 1972. They are Yvan Cournoyer, Marcel Dionne, Ken Dryden, Phil Esposito, Tony Esposito, Rod Gilbert, Guy Lapointe, Frank Mahovlich, Stan Mikita, Bobby Orr, Brad Park, Gilbert Perreault, Jean Ratelle, and Serge Savard. Coach Harry Sinden was elected as a builder.

YVAN COURNOYER
Career Summary

When Yvan Cournoyer was set to join the Montreal Canadiens for the 1964–65 season, they had a roster full of players who were all on the small side and well under the six-foot mark. The Habs weren't sure if they had room for another such winger but his great speed and shot gave Cournoyer more of a look and eventually he won over his teammates, coaches, and fans right across Canada with his great speed and skill.

When Cournoyer was 15 (and dreaming of a career with the Habs), he stood a mere five feet, three inches, and was the smallest player for the Lachine Maroons, a junior team in Quebec. Just two years later, he scored 37 goals in 42 games for the Maroons and caught the eye of the Canadiens' scouting staff. He played major junior hockey between the ages of 18 and 20 and was a prolific goal scorer (115 goals in 124 games) for the Montreal Jr. Canadiens. Cournoyer was Montreal's best junior prospect and the Habs called him up for a five-game trial during the 1963–64 season. He promptly scored four times. By this point Cournoyer had grown all the way up to five feet, seven inches, and somewhere around 160 pounds (he would fill out to a sturdy 178 as time passed), but questions about his size wouldn't go away.

Montreal coach Toe Blake always wanted his team to be a good defensive club but checking was simply not Cournoyer's game early in his career. As a result, he often found himself on the bench, called upon only when the Canadiens had a power-play opportunity or when the coach wanted a change of pace. Still he had a good hand in helping the team regain the Stanley Cup in 1965 (he scored an important goal in the seventh game of the finals versus Chicago by sweeping around Black Hawk defenceman Elmer "Moose" Vasko and then deking goalie Glenn Hall out of position). By the 1965–66 season, he was playing on a more regular basis, scoring 18 goals in 65 games. Cournoyer scored 25 in 1966–67 and, although he was still not considered a great player, he kept improving, posting 60 points (28G, 32A) in 1967–68.

Blake let Cournoyer develop slowly and was rewarded in 1968–69 when the man they called "the Roadrunner" (after a tremendously fast television cartoon character) scored 43 times.

Yvan Cournoyer brought great intensity onto the ice in his 15 full seasons with the Montreal Canadiens.

(Dennis Miles)

Cournoyer had finally learned his defensive responsibilities well enough to earn the coach's respect. He was challenged physically (by the likes of Boston's hard-nosed winger Glen Sather, for example), and while he was never going to be a fighter, Cournoyer did show he wasn't going to back down or be intimidated. The next three seasons saw him score 27, 37, and a career-high 47 goals in 1971–72, establishing himself as a consistent and respected player. By this point, he had won the Stanley Cup five times and was selected to play for Team Canada in 1972.

'72 Series Performance

Yvan Cournoyer was pretty much a fixture on the line that featured Phil Esposito and either Frank or Peter Mahovlich for many of the eight games versus the Russians. Most observers felt Cournoyer's speed would set the Soviet defenders back on their heels but the opposition seemed ready for his attacks down the wing. Although he was contained to some extent, he still produced three very important goals. The first came in the second game in Toronto when he scored a patented Cournoyer goal by flying down the wing and beating a defenceman wide before depositing a shot past Tretiak to give Canada a 2–1 lead. Canada would go on to win that game 4–1.

Cournoyer netted Canada's second goal in the sixth contest to put his team up by a 2–1 score and they went on to win that game 3–2. The next time he scored a big goal was in the last game when he and Esposito crashed the Russian net and Cournoyer picked up a loose puck and put it home to tie the game 5–5 in the third period. He was also on the ice when Paul Henderson jumped on in the last minute of the final contest. Cournoyer tried to hit his teammate with a pass, but Henderson missed it and crashed into the boards. That set Henderson up to go to the front of the Russian net when the puck ended up in the Soviet crease. Cournoyer and Esposito wouldn't come off the ice and were the first two players to reach Henderson when he scored the series-winning goal.

Cournoyer also showed another side to his game when he took on Boris Mikhailov (as close as the Russians had to a consistently nasty type of player) who had kicked teammate Gary Bergman in the seventh game. The Russian's head was pounded into the wire netting behind the net by Cournoyer but he wasn't penalized on the play. Emotionally charged was how Cournoyer played the game, which was the main reason he scored so many goals in key situations and why he was one of the most important forwards for Team Canada in 1972.

The 1972–73 season saw Cournoyer enjoy one of his best years (40G, 39A) and the Canadiens posted a league-best 52 wins and 120 points. The Habs reclaimed the Stanley Cup and Cournoyer scored his 15th goal of the playoffs in the sixth and final game of the Stanley Cup final against Chicago. There was no more doubting Cournoyer's ability to play in a big man's game. He went on to score 428 goals and 863 points in 968 games to cap off a brilliant Hall of Fame career. He was a Stanley Cup winner 10 times!

Cournoyer fences with Tim Horton, the Toronto Maple Leafs' intimidating defenceman.

Yvan Cournoyer is one of the very few players on the '72 version of Team Canada to win the Conn Smythe Trophy as the most valuable player in the Stanley Cup playoffs when he won it after his 1973 playoff performance. The other winners of the Smythe include Serge Savard (1969), Bobby Orr (1970, 1972), and Ken Dryden (1971).

TONY ESPOSITO
Career Summary

Goaltender Tony Esposito didn't like the fact that the Montreal Canadiens owned him. After attending Michigan Tech for three years, the 23-year-old Esposito felt he should have been a free agent (he was never drafted by an NHL team) with the ability to sign with any club who might want to look at him as a netminder. However, the Canadiens had been scouting him while he was in college and put his name on their negotiation list. The young netminder found the Montreal general manager, Sam Pollock, very difficult to deal with in contract talks, but he finally signed with the team before the start of the 1967–68 season. Esposito knew he needed professional experience and spent most of the '67–'68 campaign in the minors, playing 63 games for the Vancouver Canucks of the Western Hockey League, posting 25 wins.

The next season was split between the Houston Apollos (recording 10 wins in 19 appearances in the Central Hockey League) and the Canadiens (going 5–4–4 with the big league team), but there were simply too many quality goalies in the Montreal system. Rogie Vachon and Gump Worsley were Stanley Cup and Vezina Trophy winners while Phil Myre showed promise in the minors. They also had the rights to a goalie named Ken Dryden, who was developing his craft playing U.S. college hockey. Although Esposito had performed reasonably well in Montreal during the '68–'69 campaign (including two shutouts), it didn't seem as if Pollock or coach Claude Ruel were especially enthralled with his performance. Pollock left Esposito unprotected for the 1969 intra-league draft, allowing the five-foot, 11-inch, 185-pound Esposito to be selected by the Chicago Black Hawks.

The Black Hawks had missed the playoffs in '67–'68, finishing in last place in the East Division, and were looking to add new players. The Black Hawks were also fairly certain Denis DeJordy wasn't a top goaltender and were anxious to give "Tony O" a chance to be a number one netminder. As the '69–'70 season moved along Esposito piled up the shutouts and eventually set the modern-day mark when he recorded his 15th of the season — an NHL record that has yet to be tied or surpassed. Esposito hadn't only shown he was a quality goalie; he also won the Vezina Trophy and made the first all-star team for his '69–'70 performance.

Chicago was defeated by Boston in the 1970 playoffs but the Black Hawks were in the Stanley Cup finals just one year later. Chicago lost a seven-game series to Montreal despite being up 2–0 in the final game played at the Chicago Stadium. Montreal got back into the game when Jacques Lemaire beat Esposito with a long shot from just past centre ice. It was a goal that would haunt the netminder for the rest of his days since it led to the Habs coming back to win the Cup with a 3–2 victory. He bounced back to win 31 games in 1971–72, keeping him among the best goalies in the NHL. It earned him an invitation to Team Canada's training camp in 1972.

'72 Series Performance

In many ways, Tony Esposito's performance against the Russians was a great redemption for him. By the time it was over, the netminder had proven that he could win when the pressure was at its highest. Certainly, there was no greater need for a team to bounce back than the night of September 4, 1972, when the second game of the series was played at Maple Leaf Gardens. Coming off a great humiliation in Montreal, the Canadian side turned its eyes to Esposito for a much-needed great performance in goal. The game was tight and tense throughout, and in the first period, Canada had to kill off two penalties with Esposito robbing Valeri Kharlamov on one of the Russian power plays. Brother Phil scored to give Canada a 1–0 lead going into the third period and then Yvan Cournoyer scored to make it 2–0. Esposito got beaten on another Russian power play but then the Mahovlich brothers took over. Peter and Frank each scored a goal to make it 4–1 Canada, and the huge sigh of relief could be heard across the entire country!

The next two times Esposito took the net for Canada, the results were troubling. First, in Winnipeg, the Canadians were unable to hold a two-goal lead and had to settle for a 4–4 tie. The Soviets had taken just 25 shots on goal, but as usual they were opportunistic. Esposito was the goalie when the series restarted in Moscow, and for two periods everything was going

Chicago Black Hawks' goalie Tony Esposito defends his net against a Toronto Maple Leaf, with teammate and fellow Team Canada '72 alumnus Bill White pitching in. (Dennis Miles)

pretty well. Up 4–1 with 15 minutes to play, Team Canada fell apart and Esposito couldn't make a game-saving stop to stem the tide. The Russians got their game in gear and whipped four past the stunned netminder for a 5–4 victory. The Russians fired 33 shots in this game, but all Esposito could do was slam his stick on the ice after the Russians took the lead.

It wouldn't have surprised anyone if that had been the last time Esposito played in the series, with Ken Dryden and Eddie Johnston ready to go. Dryden did play in the sixth game, but it was Esposito who was back in for the all-important seventh game. Two of three goals scored by the Russians in this game came with the extra man, but Esposito was at his best in the third period with the game tied 3–3. The Russians — looking to win the series — threw 12 shots on goal in the final frame but the determined goalie only gave up one marker and then Paul Henderson scored his great goal to give Canada a thrilling 4–3 victory. Esposito won two of the biggest games in the series and gave his team a chance to win it all. He had proven he could come up big with everything on the line.

Esposito was in the Stanley Cup finals again in 1973, and although the Black Hawks lost again, he went on to record 82 career shutouts (including playoffs) and earned a place in the Hockey Hall of Fame.

Tony Esposito was one of the very few U.S. college-trained players on the Team Canada roster in 1972. The others were Red Berenson and Ken Dryden.

FRANK MAHOVLICH
Career Summary

When Frank Mahovlich was traded the first time, it came as something of a relief for the super-star left winger. For more than 10 seasons, he had been the best player on the Toronto Maple Leafs, the team that recruited him out of Northern Ontario. Despite four Stanley Cup titles and 296 goals for the Leafs, a rocky relationship with coach Punch Imlach always made life rather difficult for the man known as the "Big M." It was hoped the trade to Detroit in March 1968 would lead to Mahovlich reviving his career. In his first three seasons in Detroit, the happier Mahovlich scored 94 goals in 163 games, including a 49-goal campaign in 1968–69. He enjoyed playing alongside veteran superstars like Gordie Howe and Alex Delvecchio and that helped him adjust to his new team.

However, the Red Wings got off to a terrible start in 1970–71 and decided to make some major changes — including the trading of Mahovlich to the Montreal Canadiens despite his 14 goals and 32 points in 35 games played that year. At the time of the trade Montreal general manager Sam Pollock, one of the shrewdest dealers in NHL history, said the transaction was a "once in a lifetime deal." Montreal gave up three players (Mickey Redmond, Guy Charron, and

Frank Mahovlich tangles with the Montreal Canadiens' superstar goalie Jacques Plante.

Bill Collins) to obtain the six-foot, 205-pound Mahovlich and they never regretted the move. But when the trade was completed in February 1971, many wondered if the strong-skating Mahovlich was through being a dominant hockey player.

Mahovlich immediately started producing in Montreal, scoring 17 times and amassing 41 points in 38 games to finish the regular season. He also liked the fact that he was now team-mates with his younger brother Peter who had joined the Habs in an earlier trade. However, the Canadiens could only muster a third-place finish and faced the very tough Boston Bruins in the first round of the playoffs. The Boston side, led by league MVP Bobby Orr, was strongly favoured to oust the Canadiens but the Montreal team had other ideas. Mahovlich was able to recapture the post-season glory he had enjoyed with the Maple Leafs and that gave the Habs a chance.

The Canadiens scored more goals than expected and forced the Bruins to a seventh-game showdown in Boston. Mahovlich scored twice (including his seventh of the series) in the deciding game and Montreal hung on to win 4–2. It was one of the biggest upsets in hockey history as the 57–14–7 Bruins were knocked off by a team that had finished 24 points behind them in the regular season standings.

After beating Minnesota in the next round, the Habs had to play Chicago, the best team in the NHL's West Division, in the Stanley Cup final. Mahovlich scored a key third-period goal in the sixth game and set up his brother (with his 27th point of the playoffs) for the game winner to force another seventh game. A come-from-behind 3–2 win in Chicago two nights later gave Montreal another Stanley Cup title.

Montreal didn't win the Cup in 1972 but a 43-goal season by Mahovlich kept his name prominent among the elite of the league. He was seen as one of the leaders of Team Canada in 1972 when he was announced as one of the player selections. His big shot and long skating strides were seen as key assets in beating the Soviets.

'72 Series Performance

If there was any player on Team Canada who had great difficulty playing against the Russians, it was Frank Mahovlich. He had little respect for the communist system and always suspected there were mind games and tricks (like messing with practice times and stealing the food and beer in Moscow) being played on the Canadian players and managers that few were bringing to light. Although Mahovlich was born in Timmins, Ontario, his family roots were in Croatia, a part of the world under communist rule. He was also certain that the Russians wouldn't have agreed to play the eight-game series if they didn't think they had a chance to win. Few people associated with Team Canada thought like that at the beginning of the series but by the time the eight contests were over, it was much easier to see that Mahovlich had it right all along.

Mahovlich played in six of the eight games and was effective in the first two contests played in Montreal and Toronto where he was cheered on loudly. He assisted on the first goal of the series by Phil Esposito and then scored an insurance marker in the second game at Maple Leaf Gardens. In Winnipeg, Mahovlich lost the puck to Petrov who scored the opening goal for the Soviets to tie the game 1–1 while Canada was on a power play. He was roundly booed in Vancouver when he sat on the Russian netminder well outside the crease and that seemed to bother him for some time. Mahovlich didn't travel with the team to Sweden and was given time to collect his thoughts on his own. He didn't play in the two games against the Swedes but rejoined the squad for the Moscow games.

Mahovlich didn't register any points in game five or game eight. He was replaced, ironically enough, by his brother Peter on the line with Esposito and Yvan Cournoyer for the final period of the last game. Peter did the Mahovlich name proud with some fine work in the last 20 minutes of the series. Once the series was over, Frank skated out with his celebrating teammates in very slow fashion, likely relieved the eight games were finally over and that Canada had won. Mahovlich finished his NHL career with 533 goals and 1,103 points.

The Big M hits the boards with the Detroit Red Wings' Gordie Howe, otherwise known as Mr. Elbows.

The formation of the World Hockey Association had a big impact on the players available for Canada to select in 1972 when they signed players (like Bobby Hull) prior to the series versus the Soviets. Hull and others were ruled ineligible because they hadn't signed an NHL contract. Only three players on the Team Canada '72 roster would go on to play in the new league after the series. Those who jumped to the WHA from the '72 team included Frank Mahovlich, Paul Henderson, and Pat Stapleton.

GORDON "RED" BERENSON
Career Summary

Gordon "Red" Berenson had been around the NHL since the 1961–62 season, but his career was essentially stalled prior to the expansion of 1967. He came into the league in an unusual manner in 1961 after playing U.S. college hockey at the University of Michigan. Born in Saskatchewan, the six-foot, 185-pound Berenson had played some junior hockey with the Regina Pats (where he was considered one of the best juniors in all of Canada) and then played for the Belleville McFarlands who won the world hockey championships in 1959. He earned All-American honours at Michigan, scoring 43 goals in his final season as a Wolverine, and then signed with the Montreal Canadiens. He was a very good offensive player in the minor leagues with Hull-Ottawa and the Quebec Aces but Berenson was more of an extra player with the very talented Habs team at the big league level.

Berenson scored 23 goals in 136 games for the Canadiens and only two more in 26 playoff games, although he was with Montreal when they won the Stanley Cup in 1965. The Canadiens had to make room on their roster for some of their better prospects and sent Berenson to the New York Rangers in June 1966. The Rangers weren't nearly as deep as the Canadiens and it was thought Berenson would benefit from more ice time on Broadway. But he didn't score a goal in 30 games for New York in 1966–67 (he missed most of the year with a broken jaw) and managed just one assist in four playoff contests. He considered quitting the game but decided to give it another try. The next year saw the centre score twice in 19 games before he was traded to the expansion St. Louis Blues in November 1967. He contemplated not going to a new city once again, but realized it was his last chance to produce at the NHL level. St. Louis coach Scotty Bowman (who knew Berenson from their days together in Montreal) gave him a chance to play regularly and Berenson finished the year with 22 goals in 55 games with the Blues. By the end of the '67–'68 season Berenson was considered the first star of the NHL's West Division, which consisted of six new teams.

As soon as he arrived in St. Louis, Berenson started to show the skills that everyone assumed he had in abundance. He was a master at controlling the puck and showed more than one flashy move when he was on the attack. On the night of November 7, 1968, Berenson exceeded all expectations when he scored six times in one contest against the Philadelphia Flyers, equalling an NHL record for most goals in one game. After the game, which the Blues won 8–0, Berenson marvelled at the realization that none of his goals was a fluke. "What I liked about it is that they were all clean-cut goals, right out of the textbook. Not one rebound," he said.

Berenson would score 35 goals in 1968–69 and record 82 points in 76 games with the Blues making it to the Stanley Cup finals for the second year in a row. He scored 33 the following year, and although the Blues lost in the finals again, Berenson's playoff totals with St. Louis would show 29 points (19 of them goals) in 46 games played over his first three seasons with the team. Despite Berenson's success in St. Louis he was dealt to Detroit during the 1971–72 season, a year that saw him score 28 times and record his second-best career point total of 69. His consistent play over the previous five NHL seasons (and his previous international experience) earned him a spot on Team Canada for the '72 series.

The St. Louis Blues' Red Berenson fights off a swarm of Toronto Maple Leaf attackers.

'72 Series Performance

Red Berenson played in two games during the series with the Russians. He was on the opening night roster in Montreal and didn't appear again until the sixth game in Moscow where he registered his only point (an assist on a goal by Yvan Cournoyer). Berenson was primarily seen as a penalty killer for the '72 squad, and although he would have had lots of ice time doing that function, it was hard for coach Harry Sinden to get him into the lineup considering all the other NHL stars available to play each game. Having 35 players on the roster meant quality players like Berenson were going to have to sit out. It was an unimagined scenario at the start of the series, but the tone of it all changed once the Russian proved to be much more formidable than expected. Berenson was able to contribute in the very important sixth game because of Gilbert Perreault's decision to leave the team and return to Canada. The departure created a roster spot and for that game it was filled by the man known as "the Red Baron." Berenson also played one of the games against Sweden, a contest that ended in a 4–4 tie.

Berenson was one of the few players who played with Team Canada who didn't have a great NHL season in 1972–73 (13 goals and 43 points) but he bounced back to record 21 or more goals three more times before he retired. In all Berenson would score 261 goals and notch 658 points in 987 games played before his career ended. Berenson's good numbers helped prove that players could have a successful NHL career even if they took the college route to get there. Since that time, many college-trained players have made it to the NHL, and in some way, they should all thank Berenson.

Although all the Russian players wore helmets, only four Canadian players who appeared in the '72 series wore head protection: Red Berenson, Bill Goldsworthy, Paul Henderson, and Stan Mikita. All four players wore helmets in regular NHL play.

GILBERT PERREAULT
Career Summary

As a youngster growing up in Quebec, Gilbert Perreault had great admiration for the skill and style of the legendary Jean Beliveau, captain of the Montreal Canadiens. When Perreault had the chance, he would watch Beliveau play and practise. He would try to copy Beliveau's moves when he played hockey for the Montreal Junior Canadiens in the late 1960s. In his final two seasons of junior hockey, Perreault recorded 97 and 121 points, respectively, in leading his team to the Memorial Cup championship in back-to-back seasons. By the time his junior career was over, Perreault was the consensus best player available for the draft in June 1970. Perreault would have loved to have been taken by the Habs who were about to see the legendary Beliveau retire. However, the 1970–71 season was to be the first for the Buffalo Sabres and the Vancouver Canucks, and one of these new franchises would more than likely get the opportunity to select Perreault.

George "Punch" Imlach was in charge of the Buffalo team and he had every intention of drafting the best player available. Imlach knew lots about building winning teams (he put together teams that won four Stanley Cups in Toronto during the 1960s) and Perreault was going to be his man. A spin of a roulette wheel determined the Sabres would get to choose Perreault with the first pick of the 1970 Entry Draft. As much as Perreault would have liked to join the Canadiens, he realized that Buffalo would give him a chance to play right away. Wearing sweater number 11, Perreault carried the weight of an entire franchise on his shoulders as he went to the Sabres' first training camp. He wouldn't let the team down and the Sabres became a sporting presence on the western New York landscape.

The Buffalo team had little in terms of talent in their first year but they were going to build around Perreault who got off to a good start by leading the team in scoring in his rookie year with 72 points (including 38 goals) in 78 games played. From the moment he played in his first NHL contest Perreault was one of the most exciting players in the game. Opposing defenders would shake at the sight of the slick Sabre coming down the ice with the puck on his stick and his mouth open. He was ready to put shifty moves on any opposing player that could take him through the whole team if necessary. He could also lift the fans out of their seats the way only a few players could ever do.

In 1971–72, Perreault proved that his rookie year was no fluke by producing 74 points (26G, 48A). His good play over two seasons made him a strong choice to be selected for Team Canada even though he was only 21 years old at the time.

'72 Series Performance

Gilbert Perreault didn't get a chance to show what he could do until the fourth game of the '72 series in Vancouver. Overall, it was the worst performance of the eight games by Team Canada, but Perreault was one of the few to play well in the losing effort. The Russians jumped all over two power-play opportunities to make it 2–0. Then, early in the second period, Perreault took the puck in his own end and finished off an electrifying rush with a goal. The goal gave Canada some life, but the Soviets quickly crushed any hopes with two more goals in the second period. They would go on to win 5–3, but Perreault had shown why he was chosen for the team. Great speed, shifty moves, and an ability to finish off a good play were all the reasons he could be valuable to the team. Coach Harry Sinden liked that Perreault could give Phil Esposito, his number one centre who saw lots of action on special teams, a rest during the game.

Perreault played the first game in Moscow and did all the work to set up the first Canadian goal by Jean-Paul Parise. It looked as if Perreault was going to be in Team Canada's lineup for

Gilbert Perreault played his entire career with the expansion Buffalo Sabres. (Hockey Hall of Fame)

the rest of the series but he decided he wasn't getting enough ice time to justify staying. Sinden felt Perreault was showing a little immaturity but didn't try to talk him out of leaving. It was too bad Perreault made his choice just as he was starting to be a fixture on the team, especially since the rest of the games would be on a larger ice surface in Moscow. Perhaps he left because his good friend Rick Martin had decided to go home a little earlier and he wanted to get back to Buffalo to prepare for the upcoming NHL season. Perreault had his best NHL season to date in 1972–73 when he had 88 points, indicating that his preparation and experience with Team Canada had been worth the effort.

By the start of the 1974–75 season, the Sabres had built a team that was challenging for the best record in the league. Perreault, Martin, and right winger Rene Robert formed one of the greatest forward lines in league history. They were dubbed "the French Connection" since all three were of French-Canadian ancestry. Perreault had 96 points in just 68 games during the '74–'75 regular season and the team was ready for the playoffs like they had never been previously.

The Sabres lost the Stanley Cup to Philadelphia in a six-game series and it turned out to be the only time Perreault played in the finals during his illustrious career. The splendid centre played his entire career in Buffalo — a fitting conclusion for a man who made the Sabres franchise something special from the first day he was drafted. Gilbert Perreault would play in 1,191 career games, scoring 512 goals and recording 1,326 points. He was elected to the Hall of Fame in 1990.

The fact that Gilbert Perreault left Team Canada in the middle of the '72 series wasn't held against him when the first ever Canada Cup was played four years later in 1976. Perreault was a strong player on Team Canada '76 with eight points (4G, 4A) in seven games for the tournament-winning team. Other players on Team Canada in '72 who also played on the '76 squad included Rick Martin, Phil Esposito, Guy Lapointe, Bobby Orr, Bobby Clarke, Serge Savard, and Marcel Dionne.

STAN MIKITA
Career Summary

Stanislas Gvoth was born on May 20, 1940, in Sokolce, Czechoslovakia, just after the Second World War had begun. Gvoth was born in a small village and his parents made the most of what little they had for their family. His father, George, worked in a local factory while his mother, Emelia, farmed in the fields close to the house where they lived, giving the family a little help with the food that was in short supply. German forces invaded the country and two soldiers lived in the house for some time. They treated young Stan well even though the child had no idea why they were there or what was going on at the time.

Although he lived very modestly, Stan was like any other boy and played sports like soccer and a form of hockey. He had a pair of very rudimentary skates (blades attached to boots) and got a little idea of what hockey might be like. Eventually the Germans were defeated in the Second World War, but when the spoils of the conflict were divided after hostilities ended, the Soviet Union wound up with power over Czechoslovakia. It is quite likely young Stan would have lived out his life in his hometown but a couple of relatives had another idea.

Joe Mikita and his wife Anna had moved to Canada years ago and came back for a visit in 1948 when Stan was eight years old. A childless couple, they longed for children of their own and offered to give Stan, their nephew, a better life in Canada. It was thought the offer was something of a joke at first but the Mikitas were very serious. Stan's parents were naturally reluctant to give away a son but they also knew Stan would have a chance to live much differently across the ocean. The notion appealed to the youngster who always had a sense of adventure, and although he knew it would take him away from his real parents, Stan didn't fight the idea. He tried to forget thoughts of leaving his family but it wasn't easy. He hung on to a pole at the station and wouldn't let go but eventually the train had to leave and Stan was aboard. He was headed to Canada to live in the small town of St. Catharines, Ontario. Stanislas Gvoth had now become Stan Mikita.

He soon was playing hockey like other boys in Canada and found out he was pretty good at it. Mikita sensed resentment and hostility toward him and became a scrappy young man who always had a chip on his shoulder, but his hockey talent kept him on the straight and narrow. Soon he was signed by the Chicago Black Hawks who just happened to have their junior team in St. Catharines. Mikita was soon considered one of the best junior prospects in all of Canada. In 149 junior games with the St. Catharines TeePees, Mikita scored 85 goals and accumulated 222 points. He was ready for the NHL.

Mikita never spent a day in the minors and was on a Stanley Cup–winning team in his second full season in 1960–61. Chicago had a young and very talented team led by the likes of Mikita, Bobby Hull, Pierre Pilote, Elmer Vasko, and goalie Glenn Hall. The flashy centre finished the '61 playoffs with 11 points (6G, 5A) in 12 games and had proven to all that he was a legitimate NHL star. It was thought this might be the first championship of many for the superbly talented Chicago team but it turned out to be the only Cup team Mikita played on for the rest of his career (despite appearing in the finals again in 1965, 1971, and 1973).

By the 1963–64 season Mikita

Stan Mikita assesses the rink while the Montreal Canadiens' J.C. Tremblay hovers nearby.

won his first ever Art Ross Trophy for the most points in the regular season and he took the same trophy in 1964–65 and again in 1966–67 — a year that saw Mikita win three major awards — the Hart Trophy (MVP) and Lady Byng (most gentlemanly player) — being the others. The five-foot, nine-inch, 165-pound Mikita repeated this remarkable achievement (earning hockey's "triple crown") for the 1967–68 season as well. Mikita was 31 years old by the time of the '72 series and it was his consistent good play and point production (especially as a playmaker) that got him a spot on Team Canada.

'72 Series Performance

Stan Mikita could never seem to find the right line to play on during the '72 series and as such only played in two of the games. His first appearance came in the Toronto game where he played quite well in helping Canada to a 4–1 win. It was a very vital contest for the Canadian side and Mikita was at his feisty best. He produced his only point when he made a good play in the Soviet end of the ice to set up Frank Mahovlich for the fourth goal. Mikita dressed for the game in

Winnipeg but he didn't register a point on the scoreboard during the 4–4 tie and never suited up against the Russians again.

Mikita was most prominent in the last game Team Canada played — a contest against the Czechoslovakian national team on September 30 in Prague. He received the greatest ovation of any player when he was introduced to the crowd of 14,000 who considered him a national hero. Mikita was named team captain for this game and he nearly scored a goal but Czech goalie Jiri Holecek robbed him. Canada got a late goal to make it a 3–3 final and Mikita once again had to leave his homeland, this time after an emotional return.

Mikita had many good seasons after the '72 series, including an 83-point total in 1972–73. He scored 541 career goals and recorded 1,467 points — all for the Chicago Black Hawks.

Mikita battles with Toronto Maple Leafs goalie Bruce Gamble and defenceman Marcel Pronovost.

Stan Mikita was the only player on the 1972 team who wasn't born in Canada. In later years other players who weren't born in Canada put on the uniform with the red maple leaf on it for international play. One of those was Peter Stastny (in the 1984 Canada Cup) who was also born in Czechoslovakia. Unlike Mikita, Stastny had played his minor and junior hockey in his homeland and suited up for the Czech national team prior to playing for Team Canada.

MARCEL DIONNE
Career Summary

It was believed by his family that Marcel Dionne would grow up to be a large man like his father, Gilbert, a one-time lumberjack, who stood six foot two. But the son never grew to the height of the father and he learned to thrive in hockey at five feet, eight inches and 185 pounds. He might not have looked like a hockey player, but his scoring prowess couldn't be ignored. His diminutive stature meant Dionne would always be questioned and doubts about his ability to play in the NHL would never go away, but Dionne didn't let that stop him. He never let his size become an issue and was a great player throughout his career. He did recognize what the critics were saying about him, but Dionne let his play on the ice do all the talking.

After a stellar junior career with the St. Catharines Black Hawks of the OHA, Dionne was selected second overall by the Detroit Red Wings during the 1971 Entry Draft. Guy Lafleur, a Quebec native like Dionne, was taken first by Montreal that same year, leaving Dionne as something of an afterthought. Everyone expected Lafleur would take the NHL by storm, but it was Dionne who produced the best numbers in his first three years. As a rookie, he scored 28 goals and added 49 assists for 77 points in 78 games played. Dionne quickly showed that he was more than good enough to play in the NHL and that size wasn't going to affect his ability to create offence. Canada wanted to have young players on the team (as did the Soviets) and that made Dionne a natural for a Team Canada invite. However, Dionne felt he was invited because his agent was Alan Eagleson (who also headed the NHLPA at the time) and the team was loaded with his clients.

'72 Series Performance

As much as Team Canada wanted to give some of the rising young stars of the NHL a chance to play in the series, the coaching staff decided pretty early on that they were going to rely on the veterans to get them through the hard-fought eight-game series. The only action Dionne saw was in one tune-up game played in Stockholm against the Swedes. He was also in the lineup for the final game played in Prague before Team Canada came home. Dionne wasn't happy about how Team Canada coach Harry Sinden treated him and he didn't feel he was given a chance to show what he could do. However, he understood that it was easy to invite young players (he had just turned 21 years of age) to the training camp, and that it was just as easy to say they were too inexperienced when the going got tough. Dionne also questioned why the training camp was so chaotic at times and thought Sinden could have communicated much better with players who were sitting out.

Dionne contemplated leaving (missing one team practice) like four other players did, but he was spoken to and helped by Yvan Cournoyer and Eagleson. Those conversations made him feel better about staying through the entire series. He would later say that it was a great experience for him and his girlfriend, Carol, who later became his wife. He also observed that the Team Canada players were much more disciplined and ready to work seriously after the wives and girlfriends arrived in Moscow for the final four games of the series. Probably the best thing that happened to Dionne in September 1972 was that he was ready for the NHL season when the series was over.

He notched 90 points (including 40 goals) in 1972–73. In his fourth NHL season, he recorded 121 points for a brutal Detroit team. The fact is Dionne never warmed up to Detroit management or coaching and was openly outspoken that the Red Wings had only Nick Libbett, Mickey Redmond, Danny Grant, Gary Bergman, and himself as legitimate NHL-quality players. When the Los Angeles Kings offered him a large contract, Dionne jumped at the opportunity to go out to the West Coast and leave the Red Wings behind. Unfortunately the Kings were never really that much better than the Red Wings, but he did get into 43 playoff games for the Kings between 1976 and 1987, recording 20 goals and 44 points. Dionne became one of the greatest stars in the game. He maintained his quick, shifty demeanour on the ice and his touch around the net would only get better in Los Angeles. He would score 50 or more goals and record 100 or more points six times while with the Kings. Eventually he was teamed with wingers Dave Taylor and Charlie Simmer, forming a trio that became known as the "Triple Crown Line." The line was a constant scoring threat to any opposing team.

In 1979–80, Dionne showed that he could be the leader in NHL scoring despite being on a rather average team. He led the Triple Crown Line to a great year as he recorded a league-best 137 points, while Simmer scored a league-high 56 (tied with two others) goals, and Taylor racked up 90 points. Dionne was actually tied in points with a rookie named Wayne Gretzky but was awarded the Art Ross Trophy based on goal totals (53 to 51). It was the only time Dionne would lead the NHL in points, as Gretzky and Mario Lemieux dominated the scoring race for the next 16 years.

While there were no championships for Dionne, he did finish his illustrious career with the New York Rangers by playing two years on Broadway. His time in the NHL ended with 731 goals (fourth all-time) and 1,771 points (fifth all-time) in 1,384 games played.

Marcel Dionne's Team Canada '72 playing card — Dionne was just starting his illustrious career with the Detroit Red Wings when he got the call to participate in the Summit Series. (Future Trends Experience Ltd.)

Marcel Dionne never had the opportunity to show what he could do for Team Canada in 1972. However, between the ages of 25 and 34, Dionne represented Canada in international play six times. He also played in two games of the 1979 Challenge Cup for the NHL All-Stars in a three-game series versus the Russians. Wayne Gretzky represented Canada a total of eight times (between the ages of 21 and 37) after he turned professional.

BOBBY ORR
Career Summary

The Boston Bruins organization went on a trip in the spring of 1960 in a much-needed search for new hockey talent. They had been tipped about a couple of youngsters playing bantam hockey for a team from Parry Sound, Ontario, and were anxious to see these two boys play in a tournament in Gananoque, Ontario, about 20 miles from the city of Kingston. The Boston management staff and scouts spread themselves over the entire arena so they could all get different points of view. When they gathered to discuss what they had seen in the first period of the game, the two players they had been told to watch weren't even mentioned. Instead, all the Bruins scouts agreed that a five-foot, two-inch, 110-pound defenceman wearing sweater number 2 was the most outstanding player.

However, they didn't even know who he was and they had to make inquiries. Soon they learned his name was Bobby Orr and he was just 12 years old. The next question was whether the team from Parry Sound was sponsored by any of the other five NHL teams. Luckily for the Bruins the answer was no and soon the chase to secure the talented defenceman for the last-place Boston club was on full throttle. Wren Blair made it his personal crusade to sign Orr for the Bruins, and at the age of 14, the boy was in the Boston organization.

As Orr was set to turn professional as an 18-year-old, the expectations for him had already become enormous. His first two seasons (starting in 1966–67) were shortened because of a knee injury, but Orr and the Bruins rapidly improved. By his third year, he had 64 points (21G, 43A) in 67 games played and had become the most dominant player in the game. The 1969–70 season saw Orr lead the entire league in points (120) and he won virtually all the major awards (including best defencemen and most valuable player in the league). The Bruins had been getting better in the playoffs and in the 1970 post-season they easily defeated New York and Chicago to make it to the Stanley Cup finals against the St. Louis Blues.

The Bruins were up 3–0 in games with the fourth contest scheduled for the Boston Garden on the afternoon of May 10, 1970. The St. Louis Blues were really no match for the Bruins but on this hot and steamy day they weren't going down without a fight. The game went into overtime with the score tied 3–3. The Bruins stormed out for the extra session and got the puck deep in the Blues' end. Sensing the moment was at hand, Orr charged in from the blueline as teammate Derek Sanderson had the puck behind the St. Louis net. A perfect pass to the hard-charging

Although he was officially on Team Canada '72, Bobby Orr never got to play due to injury. However, here he works furiously behind the Maple Leafs' net, with Toronto Bob Pulford casting a wary eye.

defenceman right in front of the net resulted in a quick, deadly, accurate shot by Orr that Blues netminder Glenn Hall had no chance to stop. The Bruin saviour leapt into the air as he tripped over the stick of St. Louis defenceman Noel Picard. When he landed on the ice, Orr had fulfilled his destiny and the Bruins were champions for the first time in 29 years!

If that wasn't enough, Orr saved the Bruins once again in the 1972 final against the New York Rangers. The Bruins had failed to wrap the series in five games when they had a chance on home ice and now had to face the prospect of winning on Broadway. It was a close, hard-fought contest, but in the end, the difference was Orr who once again scored the Cup winner and assisted on another goal scored by Wayne Cashman, helping to make it a 3–0 final for the Bruins. He won his second Conn Smythe Trophy for his performance in the playoffs and was clearly the best player in the NHL. He was the first player anyone would have mentioned when selecting Team Canada for the '72 series.

'72 Series Performance

In June 1972, just after the Bruins had won the Stanley Cup, Orr had knee surgery, but it was hoped he could come back in time for the series versus the Russians. Orr gave it his best try but his knee would need more time to recover. He was at training camp and tried skating with the team but he was clearly labouring. Although nobody expected him to play in the games in Canada, there was some thought that Orr could maybe suit up for the games in Moscow. However, after he was unable to dress for the games Team Canada played in Sweden (his knee swelled up after a workout), it was decided at that point he wouldn't play against the Russians. For such a competitive player as Orr, the news was heartbreaking and there is no doubt he would have made a big difference in the series had he been able to play. Team Canada could have used Orr's puck-carrying ability to get themselves out of trouble in their own end but his absence gave others an opportunity they might not have otherwise received.

Orr returned to NHL action in the 1972–73 season and in just 63 games played, he had 29 goals and 101 points. Despite knee woes that plagued him throughout his career, Orr was able to put in three more great seasons before his injury caused him to play very infrequently. He got the Bruins to the final once again in 1974, but the Philadelphia Flyers, led by Bobby Clarke, won the Stanley Cup in six games. His final full NHL season saw him record 135 points (the most of any player in 1974–75), which helped earn him another Norris Trophy, the eighth of his illustrious career. By 1979–80, he was forced to retire, no longer able to play with his aching knees.

Although Bobby Orr was unable to play in the '72 series, he was able to compete for Team Canada in 1976 for the first ever Canada Cup Tournament. Playing essentially on one leg, Orr was named the outstanding player of the '76 tournament with nine points in seven games played. It was his last dominating performance. If Orr had played in '72, it is quite likely he would have received consideration as the best Canadian player but instead that honour was divided between Paul Henderson and Phil Esposito. Both players received a new car in recognition of their award.

PETER MAHOVLICH
Career Summary

The Toronto Maple Leafs were very interested in uniting Peter Mahovlich with his brother Frank (a legendary performer for Toronto from the minute he played his first game) on the same team. They were ready to select the gangly but talented centre in the 1963 Amateur Draft (the first ever held by the NHL) with the fifth pick, but Detroit snapped Mahovlich up with the second choice thus ending the Leafs' hope of having the brothers together. Peter was nine years younger than Frank, and the Red Wings had had their eyes on him for some time. Peter was assigned to the Hamilton Red Wings junior team where he produced 138 points in 155 games played. He was never a smooth player and at times a little out of control (121 penalty minutes during his last year in Hamilton), but could score some memorable goals and displayed an ability to shift his body in almost any direction.

But the large (six-foot, five-inch, 210-pound) centre couldn't adjust to the NHL fast enough as far as the Red Wings were concerned. He played in the minors where he produced at a good clip (more than a point per game pace), but found the big league a harder place to enjoy the same kind of success (only 15 goals scored over parts of three years with Detroit). Montreal

Peter Mahovlich, here with the Detroit Red Wings, is squeezed
by Tim Horton and Bob Pulford (20) of the Toronto Maple Leafs.

offered Gary Monahan, the only player chosen ahead of Mahovlich in 1963, in exchange for the still-young prospect in June 1969 and never came to regret the move.

After some more time in the minors, Mahovlich soon became a regular in Montreal and listened when teammate John Ferguson told him to use his body more. He put together back-to-back 35-goal seasons. A little while later, brother Frank was acquired by the Canadiens. The pair helped lead the Canadiens to a surprising Stanley Cup in 1971, both scoring key goals all through the playoffs. Peter might have been a somewhat surprising choice for Team Canada in '72 but those in the know could see he had finally come of age.

'72 Series Performance

Peter Mahovlich missed only one game of the '72 series and recorded a couple of points. His play throughout the series was very good but his main contribution came at three key moments and they were undeniable. The first came in Toronto when Team Canada was trying to protect a 2–1 lead but had to kill off a penalty. Phil Esposito whacked the puck out of the Canadian end by putting it off the boards, and the black disc came to Mahovlich who suddenly found himself up against one Soviet defenceman, Yevgeny Poladiev. Mahovlich teased the Russian defender with the puck before sliding it past him with a deft move to the inside. He then barrelled in on goalie Tretiak and got the Soviet netminder to go down before backhanding the puck home as he ran over the Russian netminder. The crowd at Maple Leaf Gardens erupted like never before, and the players on Team Canada came over the boards to congratulate a deliriously happy Mahovlich.

Another important play made by Mahovlich came in the third period of the last game with Canada down 5–3. He replaced his brother on the line with Esposito and Yvan Cournoyer and set up the first goal of the Canadian comeback by Esposito just 2:27 into the final frame. It was a very important goal since it came early in the period and gave Canada a chance to gain some momentum. Cournoyer tied the game and then Mahovlich made the best assist of all when he came off the ice to let Paul Henderson on to score the winner. "Pete! Pete," screamed Henderson and luckily, Mahovlich was listening, making it back to the bench in time for the hero of the series to score with just 34 seconds to play!

Mahovlich recorded 59 points in 61 games in 1972–73 and added 13 points in 17 playoff games to get the Stanley Cup back for Montreal. He would go on to win two more Stanley Cups with Montreal and twice recorded more the 100 points in the regular season. He also played for Pittsburgh before returning to Detroit for two final seasons of NHL play. His final point tally was 773 (288G, 485A) in 884 career games — excellent numbers for a player few were sure about when he first started in the NHL.

When Peter Mahovlich got past defenceman Yevgeny Poladiev, it was a play that the Russian coaches took note of and number 26 for the Soviets appeared in only one more game (the fourth in Vancouver) during the series after playing in the first two. After the loss in Toronto, the Russians made changes to their lineup and inserted three players (Vyacheslav Anisin, Alexander Bodunov, and Yuri Lebedev), all aged 21 and making their first international hockey appearance. Coach Harry Sinden was credited with making many good roster moves for Canada but Russian coaches Boris Kulagin and Vsevolod Bobrov also showed they could alter their team lineup effectively.

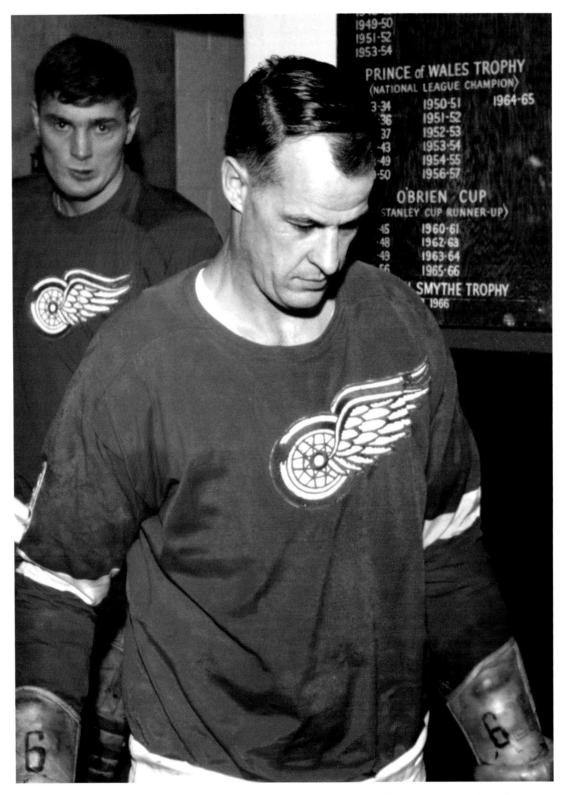

Peter Mahovlich follows Gordie Howe out into the arena.

SERGE SAVARD
Career Summary

Serge Savard was first noticed by the Montreal Canadiens when he was just 15 years of age and was playing hockey for his school team. Savard's father was a great hockey fan and he was pleased the native of Montreal was looked upon favourably by the Canadiens. The Habs put his name on their negotiation list but he didn't make the Montreal Junior Canadiens on his first try. Sent back to Junior B, the lean and lanky (six-foot, two-inch, 210-pound) Savard showed improvement in his game and now focused on playing defence where he was much better suited and more valuable. He was developed under the watchful eye of Scotty Bowman after he made the Junior Canadiens and he got plenty of ice time when he was 18 and 19 years old. His final year of junior saw him record 47 points in 56 games, an indication he was going to be an all-round defenceman.

Although Savard played in two games of the 1966–67 season with Montreal, he spent most of the year with the Houston Apollos of the Central Hockey League to get some time in as a professional. When the Habs lost the '67 Stanley Cup final, they were prepared to implement changes to their big league roster for the next season. Savard played his first full year in the NHL and recorded 15 points in 67 games. Montreal recaptured the Cup in 1968 and won it again in 1969 — a postseason that saw the young Savard play a major role in Montreal winning the championship. His performance in the playoffs was so outstanding (10 points in 14 games) that Savard was named the winner of the Conn Smythe Trophy (the first defenceman to win) at the tender age of 23. Two severe injuries to his leg over the next two seasons set Savard back, but in 1971–72, he returned to play 23 games and thought his invite to Team Canada was more or less to fill out the roster. It turned out his selection was one of the best made by Team Canada.

'72 Series Performance

Serge Savard wasn't in the lineup on opening night in Montreal, but when the 7–3 loss was reviewed, the Canadian team turned to him for help on the staggering blueline. He quickly showed why he was so important by lugging the puck out of the Canadian end and playing his usually sound defensive game. The team gained more confidence with his calming presence on the ice and he paired very effectively with fellow Habs defenceman Guy Lapointe. He didn't contribute any points in the second and third games of the series, but Canada didn't lose either contest.

However, as the team worked out in Vancouver before the fourth game, Savard suffered a hairline fracture in his ankle (stopping a shot by Red Berenson in practice) and was feeling terrible about another leg injury — this time to his left ankle. Coach Harry Sinden announced that Savard was through for the series but somehow the defenceman got ready and played in

Serge Savard was one of the NHL's all-time premier defencemen.
He won eight Stanley Cups with the Montreal Canadiens.

the final three games of the series in Moscow. In the seventh game of the series, Savard picked up two key assists to help Canada win 4–3 to force the final game showdown. His first helper came on a goal by Phil Esposito in the first period that tied the game 2–2. His second assist on the night was even more important because it help set up Paul Henderson for his spectacular winning goal while the teams were playing four-on-four hockey. He didn't register a point in the eighth game, but his great play was very much needed by Team Canada to secure a very close 6–5 victory. To top off his great performance, Savard scored two goals in the game against Czechoslovakia, including the one that tied the score 3–3 with just four seconds to play. Savard never lost a game in which he suited up for Team Canada in 1972.

Savard had a very good year in 1972–73 with 39 points (including 32 assists), and Montreal went on to win the Stanley Cup once more with the rangy blueliner recording 11 points in 17 playoff games. One of Savard's proudest moments in the NHL came when the Canadiens defeated the Philadelphia Flyers in four straight games during the 1976 Stanley Cup final. Savard strongly believed that the Flyers' brawling style of hockey was bad for the game and the Habs showed that skill (with some toughness) was always going to beat pure brawn.

He would win four more championships (bringing his total to eight — including the '71 championship when he missed the entire playoffs) as a player before retiring after two seasons as a Winnipeg Jet. Savard then won two Stanley Cups (in 1986 and 1993) as the general manager of the Montreal Canadiens — a perfect way to conclude his glorious stay in hockey.

> Serge Savard is one of seven players or coaches on the '72 Team Canada to go on to become an NHL general manager. The others were Harry Sinden, John Ferguson, Phil Esposito, Eddie Johnston, Tony Esposito, Ken Dryden, and Bobby Clarke. In 2012, Savard was named an executive vice-president of the Canadiens.

GUY LAPOINTE
Career Summary

Defenceman Guy Lapointe was one of the last players the Montreal Canadiens were able to recruit before the start of the universal draft. It was a good thing the Habs were able to secure Lapointe before the draft started because if they hadn't done so, many NHL teams would have been interested in the services of the six-foot, 205-pound blueliner. Lapointe actually wanted to be a firefighter like his brother but was persuaded to try pro hockey when the Canadiens came calling.

At the age of 17, Lapointe played for the Verdun Maple Leafs during the 1965–66 season (20 points in 37 games) and then moved up to the Montreal Junior Canadiens when he turned 19 in 1967–68 (38 points in 51 games). While his numbers may not have been spectacular, he was developing his all-round game quite nicely, and Lapointe turned pro with the Houston Apollos in 1968–69 when he was 20 years of age. He went to Nova Scotia to play for the Voyageurs the next year and had an impressive 38 points in 51 contests. He also managed to get into six games for Montreal over the same two seasons but didn't register a point.

By the 1970–71 campaign, the Habs felt Lapointe was ready for the big league and he impressed with 15 goals and 29 assists in 78 games played, while recording a plus 28 mark.

In the 1970s the Montreal Canadiens had perhaps the most formidable defence troika ever to skate in the NHL. Larry Robinson and Serge Savard were two of those matchless defenders; the other was Guy Lapointe, number 5.

[Dennis Miles]

His performance indicated that Montreal had once again developed a prospect the right way. When injury kept Serge Savard out of the '71 playoffs, Lapointe stepped up and became a star. In 20 post-season games, he had nine points (including four goals), and contributed greatly to the Habs pulling off a couple of upsets to take the Stanley Cup in an unexpected fashion. He played in only 69 games in 1971–72 but managed to get more points (44) than he had the year before. When Team Canada selections were being considered his veteran Montreal teammates got the first look, but when J.C. Tremblay and Jacques Laperriere were both unavailable, Team Canada decided to go with another Hab and named Lapointe to the squad despite his lack of experience and his relative youth at the age of 24.

'72 Series Performance

It would have been understandable if Lapointe had said no to his Team Canada invite since his wife was expecting their first child. However, he was in the lineup for the first game in Montreal, but it didn't go well for Team Canada or for Lapointe. He was very aggressive in the Montreal contest and as the game wore on, he was taking runs at Russian players he normally wouldn't have contemplated. He was penalized late in the game, but he could have had other hits on Soviet players called on him. Lapointe is still emotional about the opening loss to the Russians (perhaps in part because it took place in his hometown), but he got better quickly, especially when Savard joined the active roster for the next game in Toronto.

Soon Lapointe and Savard steadied Team Canada along the blueline and gave their team a chance to win — most noticeably in Moscow. Lapointe and Savard both missed the game in Vancouver with injuries and their absence was very noticeable. Lapointe was able to return for the fifth game in Moscow (a 5–4 loss) and felt better when he was sure his wife (who gave birth while the team was in Sweden) and newborn son were both doing well. He gained more confidence when Savard returned for the remaining three games in the Soviet Union. There the two defencemen were essential to Canada taking all three games in a must-win scenario. Lapointe recorded one point in the series (an assist on a goal by Paul Henderson in the fifth game), but his contribution to the ultimate series victory went well beyond what he provided in points. Late in the eighth game with less than two minutes to play, Lapointe belted Yakushev, the most dangerous Russian on the night who had already scored twice, with a solid bodycheck, keeping the Soviet winger away from the Canadian net.

After the '72 series was over Lapointe went on to have a stellar career with the Canadiens, starting with the 1972–73 season when he had 19 goals and 54 points. Lapointe and the Habs won the Stanley Cup that year and he was on the great Hab teams that won the championship in 1976, 1977, 1978, and 1979. His great shot from the point helped him to score 21 or more goals three times (28 was his highest total in 1974–75) and Lapointe was an NHL all-star four times (once on the first team). His 884 games included some in St. Louis and Boston at the end of his career, but he will always be recalled as one the great Montreal Canadiens players of all time. He was elected to the Hockey Hall of Fame in 1993.

> A big part of the reason Team Canada was able to come back and win the 1972 series was the pairing of Guy Lapointe and Serge Savard. They didn't lose a game they played together. Among the other Canadian defensive pairings during the series were Gary Bergman and Brad Park and Pat Stapleton and Bill White. Going with three pairs and six defencemen gave Canada a decided edge in how they were going to defend against the Russians. Most NHL teams at that time were usually going with five blueliners, but Coach Harry Sinden's decision to play with six was vital to Canada taking the series 4–3–1.

ROD SEILING
Career Summary

Rod Seiling was just a kid of 19 when he found out he had been traded from the Toronto Maple Leafs to the New York Rangers on February 22, 1964. Nobody from the Leafs organization called him to tell him the news. Instead, he heard about it on the radio and was as surprised as anyone to learn he was involved in a seven-player swap. Seiling was part of the Toronto Marlboros (the Leafs junior affiliate) at the time of the deal and was considered the best prospect in all of Canada. The Marlies were a powerful team and the Rangers left Seiling (who recorded 100 points in 60 games played — including playoffs — as a junior in 1963–64) in Toronto even after they had acquired his rights. It was a good decision by New York to leave Seiling there since the Marlies went on to win the Memorial Cup in 1964. It also made the young defenceman feel a little better as he left the Leafs organization and made his way to the Rangers who weren't a strong team at the time while Toronto was winning Stanley Cups.

The Rangers did want a quick look at Seiling and called him up for two games prior to the end of the '63–'64 campaign. He made a distinct impression by throwing a heavy bodycheck at Chicago defenceman Pierre Pilote at Madison Square Garden. Seiling's hit got the crowd on his side and the Rangers went on to win the game 4–3. He played another game in Montreal and the New York club recorded a 3–2 upset of the mighty Habs. Seiling picked up one assist in the two games and showed he was going make a solid contribution to his new team.

The Rangers had given up two good players (captain Andy Bathgate and veteran wing Don McKenney who helped the Leafs win the Cup in '64) to get Seiling along with Arnie Brown, Dick Duff, Bob Nevin, and Bill Collins. The Maple Leafs did well immediately, but in the long term, the Rangers had made a pretty good deal. Seiling made the New York club without heading to the minors and produced a good number of assists every season but not so many goals. Although Seiling wasn't small (six feet tall, 190 pounds), he relied on his finesse skills to get the most out of his abilities. Injuries slowed him down for a couple of years but as the Rangers got better Seiling became a more highly valued member of the team. By 1969–70 he was considered one of the steadiest defencemen in the NHL and his plus/minus total was always among the best (he was a plus 53 in 1971–72). Seiling had one of his best years in '71–'72 when he had five goals and 36 assists for 41 points and the Rangers made it to the Stanley Cup finals. Those good numbers and the Rangers' performance made Seiling a strong candidate for Team Canada.

'72 Series Performance

Rod Seiling's performance in the Canada-Russia series might be best summarized with the phrase "wrong place, wrong time." Seiling made the opening night lineup in Montreal and was teamed with Boston defenceman Don Awrey. The pair of veteran blueliners faded as the game went along and looked far too slow to keep up with the fast Russian forwards. The real damage inflicted by the Russians came late in the game when they popped in three quick goals to make it a 7–3 final but the perception was that Seiling and Awrey were the least effective pairing on the ice for Team Canada.

The pairing was used again in the Vancouver game and the Russians once more made many on Team Canada look bad during a 5–3 loss. Seiling would get one more chance to redeem

Rod Seiling is best-known as a New York Ranger, but he also played for the Toronto Maple Leafs, the Washington Capitals, the St. Louis Blues, and the Atlanta Flames.

himself in Moscow, but the Canadian side blew a 4–1 lead in the third period before losing 5–4. Seiling didn't play a great deal in this game, but it was he and Bobby Clarke who lost the puck on the winning goal by Vladimir Vikulov. The unexpected loss by Canada practically forced coach Harry Sinden to go with his strongest defensive pairings, and that meant Guy Lapointe and Serge Savard were going to go back in after they recovered from injuries. Seiling didn't play in the remaining three games. Team Canada didn't win a game Seiling appeared in, but, while his play wasn't outstanding (no points), he was no more at fault in the three defeats than his teammates were. Physical conditioning may have been a factor for many Canadian players in this series and Seiling was no exception. NHL players were simply not ready to play meaningful hockey in September.

Even though his experience with Team Canada wasn't the best, Seiling returned to New York and produced a 42-point season (his highest total in the NHL) in 1972–73. His last full season in New York (he was on Broadway for 12 years) saw Seiling record 30 points in 68 games and the Rangers nearly made it to the finals before losing a tough seven-game series to the Philadelphia Flyers. Seiling played in Washington, Toronto, St. Louis, and Atlanta before his 979-game career ended.

> Rod Seiling was the only member of Team Canada in 1972 that would see a younger brother play in the NHL in the future. Ric Seiling (born 13 years after his older sibling) was drafted 14th overall by the Buffalo Sabres in 1977. The brothers both played in the league for two seasons before Rod retired.

JOCELYN GUEVREMONT
Career Summary

When the 1971 NHL Entry Draft was held all the talk was about the first two players taken. Guy Lafleur went first overall to Montreal while Marcel Dionne was selected second by the Detroit Red Wings. The second-year Vancouver Canucks were picking third and they made defenceman Jocelyn Guevremont their choice. A large man at six feet, two inches, and 200 pounds, Guevremont had enjoyed a very good junior career when he played in his hometown of Montreal for the Junior Canadiens. He was on two back-to-back Memorial Cup teams (1969, 1970) with the junior Habs on a team that featured other future NHL greats like Gilbert Perreault, Rick Martin, Rejean Houle, Marc Tardiff, and Ian Turnbull among others. Guevremont was a point-a-game defenceman during his entire time in junior and the fact that he won championships made him a very attractive commodity to the Canucks who were looking to build their team with a solid group of defencemen.

Guevremont almost never made it to the NHL because as a youngster he played forward and was too slow to stay up front. When he was 14 years old, a coach told Guevremont he wasn't going anywhere as a forward and was going to be replaced. The youngster sensed that the coach was serious and quickly asked if he could move back to play along the blueline. His coach readily agreed and just three years later, he was a star for the Junior Canadiens. It was Guevremont's dream to play for the Montreal Canadiens in the NHL and he was often compared to Jacques Laperriere, a Hall of Fame defenceman for the Habs during the 1960s and 1970s. Guevremont wasn't quite as good as the stellar Laperriere but he was good in his own end and could shoot the puck with anybody in hockey from the blueline. He never played a game in the minors, as he was just 20 years old when he started his rookie year in the NHL for Vancouver. He scored 13 times and recorded 51 total points in 75 games played. The Canucks were still a bad team in '71–'72 and finished last in the East Division of the NHL with just 20 wins and a total of 48 points. He was invited to be a part of Team Canada in 1972 but it was clear he was asked to do so because it was determined Vancouver should have two players on the Canadian roster (the other was Dale Tallon). Guevremont was fairly certain he wasn't going to play in the games against Russia but said he would participate and looked forward to a trip to the Soviet Union — a great experience for someone who was just 21 years old.

'72 Series Performance

As he knew beforehand, Jocelyn Guevremont wouldn't play in any of the eight games against Russia (not even in the Vancouver game played on September 8, 1972). He did get into both games Team Canada played in Sweden but his ice time in those contests was still rather limited and he didn't record a point. When the team arrived in Moscow for the remaining four games, it was difficult for the players not suiting up because they couldn't even practise. Many became bored and upset with the lack of opportunity and Guevremont was one of four players who decided to return home and get ready for the NHL season.

At the time of his departure, it was said that Guevremont wanted to get back to the Vancouver training camp but he later said that he returned home because his wife was ill and he wanted to attend to her needs. The story about his wife not feeling well wasn't the one making the rounds among the press and he and the other three were unfairly labelled as deserters. Guevremont felt that some players on Team Canada may have held his departure against him but that was by no means the consensus.

Even though Guevremont had a very good rookie season, it was still a surprise that he was invited to Team Canada. Coach Harry Sinden called the invite to Guevremont something political — as in they wanted Canuck players involved to help sell tickets for the Vancouver contest — but it was another indicator of how Canada wasn't really prepared for this series to be anything but an easy victory.

Guevremont scored 16 goals in his second year and 15 in his third — both high totals for defencemen in this era — but for some reason the Canucks soured on his play and dealt him to Buffalo early in the 1974–75 season. The Sabres made it to the Stanley Cup finals that year before losing to Philadelphia, and Guevremont was a steady performer for the Buffalo club. He had his best year as a Sabre when he had 52 points in 80 games during the 1975–76 season, although a very talented Sabre team never made it back to the finals again. Guevremont's career lasted 571 games and finished with a small stint (20 games) as a New York Ranger in 1979–80.

The universal draft began in 1969 and a few members of Team Canada were first-round draft picks. They included Gilbert Perreault (first overall in 1970), Dale Tallon (second overall in 1970), Marcel Dionne (second overall in 1971), Rick Martin (fifth overall in 1971), and Jocelyn Guevremont (third overall in 1971).

VIC HADFIELD
Career Summary

Vic Hadfield was always a very tough hockey player. In 1963–64 he led the entire NHL with 151 penalty minutes and it was just his first full season in the league! The rangy left winger had started his career with the Chicago Black Hawks organization where he was part of a Memorial Cup–winning team when he played with the St. Catharines Teepees in the 1959–60 season. Some of his teammates on the Teepees included future NHL players like Roger Crozier, Ray Cullen, John Brenneman, Murray Hall, Doug Robinson, Chico Maki, and '72 Team Canada member Pat Stapleton. Hadfield racked up 73 points but also put up 202 penalty minutes over two seasons in St. Catharines.

Hadfield began his professional career in the minors playing for the Buffalo Bisons where he recorded 21 points and 111 penalty minutes. The Black Hawks may have felt Hadfield would be nothing more than a tough guy and left him available during the 1961 intra-league draft. He was quickly snapped up by the New York Rangers who were looking for good young talent and some toughness. At six feet and 185 pounds, the native of Oakville, Ontario, was one of the bigger Ranger forwards and he was always willing to use his size effectively. As a rookie, he was best known for the time he spent in the penalty box but Hadfield also scored 14 goals — an impressive total in the era of the "Original Six." The Rangers weren't a very good team until the 1966–67 season when they finally made it back to the playoffs. Montreal easily swept the Rangers aside in four games but players like Hadfield had clearly given the New York team a new look.

Rangers coach and general manager Emile Francis eventually placed Hadfield on a line with Rod Gilbert and Jean Ratelle. The trio clicked on all aspects of the game, racking up goals and points at a very good rate. They became known as the G-A-G Line (or goal-a-game) and were a dominating trio. The Rangers were now perennial contenders (making the playoffs for five straight campaigns) and the 1971–72 season saw Hadfield produce his best year with 50 goals (the first Ranger to ever do so) and 106 points. New York made it to the Stanley Cup finals for the first time since 1950 but lost in six games to the Boston Bruins led by Bobby Orr. The G-A-G Line had played so well that all three players were invited to play for Team Canada in 1972 — a move that made sense if the three were allowed to play together.

'72 Series Performance

The New York Rangers' forward line, which featured Vic Hadfield on left wing, Rod Gilbert on right wing, and the classy Jean Ratelle at centre, started the '72 series in Montreal but took a great deal of the heat for the 7–3 loss at the hands of the Soviet Union. Hadfield tried to play in his usual rugged manner, but it wasn't effective in slowing down the smaller Russian forwards who could all skate very fast. Hadfield wasn't in the lineup again until the series moved to Vancouver. Gilbert was alongside, but Ratelle (who had played in Winnipeg) was missing from the fourth-game roster. This bothered Hadfield a great deal, and he spent too much time trying to rough up the Russians, although he was certainly not the only Canadian player guilty of this in the fourth game.

The next part of the '72 experience for Hadfield was especially difficult when the team played a couple of games in Sweden to get ready for the larger-sized international ice rink. Hadfield said he was speared in the first game, and whacked a Swede across the ankle in retaliation. In the

New York Ranger Vic Hadfield duels with the Chicago Black Hawks' Wayne Hillman.

second game, it got uglier. He was slashed across the arm and came back at Lars-Erik Sjoberg with a stick across the face. The Swede's nose was broken and he bled all over the ice before going in for repairs. Sjoberg (who would go on to play in the WHA and NHL with Winnipeg) stared at Hadfield as he sat in the penalty box but the Canadian player showed no emotion as the Swedish player bled profusely in front of the cameras.

It soon became obvious to Hadfield that he wasn't a favourite of coach Harry Sinden. After a disagreement at a Moscow practice, he decided to leave and return to New York for the start of the new NHL season. There was likely little chance of Hadfield getting back into the lineup so his decision to leave, although it was met with tremendous scorn in Canada, was the right one at the time. The larger ice surface would likely have been too much of a problem for Hadfield, who was a bit of a lumbering skater, and his apparent short fuse would have been an issue as well. His relationship with Sinden was to say the least strained at the time and that wasn't going to benefit him at all for the four games in Moscow.

Hadfield never scored 50 goals again but he did put up seasons of 28, 27, 31, and 30 before he called it a career. He was dealt to the Pittsburgh Penguins where he played out the final three years of his 1,002-game career. He finished with 323 goals and 712 points — impressive totals for someone who was just supposed to be tough!

Vic Hadfield was one of five players on Team Canada '72 who recorded at least one 50-goal season while they played in the NHL. The others were Phil Esposito, Marcel Dionne, Mickey Redmond, and Rick Martin.

BRAD PARK
Career Summary

It seemed that defenceman Brad Park was always thought of as the second best. First, it was as a youngster when his older (by two years) brother Ron would get more of the attention when he played hockey. One time Park volunteered to play in net for his brother's team just to get into action when the regular goalie had to miss a game. Brad gave up an early goal but then shut out the other team the rest of the way. It helped Park that his father was coaching teams he played on through much of his hockey development. He got to play in the very prestigious Quebec International Peewee tournament and won the championship game. His father emphasized a puck control game and wanted his son to be physical whenever possible. The young defence-man learned his lessons well.

When his father had to move back to Toronto (where Brad was born) because of his job, Park landed on the Neil MacNeil High School team, a club that fed players to the Toronto Marlboros junior team. The next year, the high school team folded and Brad was offered a tryout for the Junior A team in Hamilton. However, the Marlboros wanted Park for their team even though they weren't totally convinced he could play for them at the highest level. When it came time to show what he could do at a tryout, Park made the team and he was with the Marlies when they won the Memorial Cup in 1967 with one of the best teams ever assembled. Park should have been the property of the Toronto Maple Leafs, but they hadn't signed him, so he was eligible for the 1966 Amateur Draft where he was scooped up by the New York Rangers. He played fewer than 20 games in the minors (14 points in 17 contests) in 1968–69 before the Rangers put him on the big team and he became a permanent fixture there.

In short order Park became one of the top defencemen in the NHL. He was producing more assists than goals but in the 1969–70 season, when he had 11 goals and 26 assists, he was named to the first all-star team — right next to Bobby Orr. The comparisons to Orr wouldn't go away

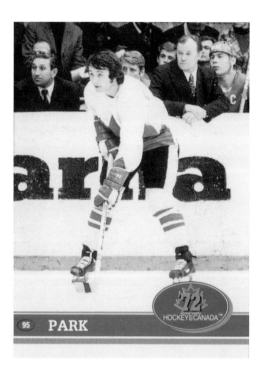

Brad Park's Team Canada '72 playing card. Principally with the New York Rangers and the Boston Bruins, defenceman Park racked up an impressive number of career goals (213) and assists (683) in the regular season. (Future Trends Experience Ltd.)

for Park but he learned to accept his place in the NHL with a good sense of humour. He always thought that being number two to Orr was actually flattering!

Park was outstanding in 1970–71 when he raised his point total to 44 but it was his performance the following year, in 1971–72, that really captured the attention of everyone in hockey. He had a 73-point season and was a first-team all-star once more. However, it was the Boston Bruins who defeated the Rangers in the Stanley Cup final with Orr winning the Conn Smythe (Orr also won the Norris Trophy as the league's best defenceman). Park had been runner-up to Orr three times for the Norris but number two was always trying harder. Everyone was looking forward to seeing Park and Orr man the points on the power play for Team Canada in 1972. Park also became a father while the team was still in Canada and that might have been something of a distraction as he prepared for the series.

'72 Series Performance

Brad Park had difficulty adjusting to the Russian style of attack in the early going of the series and wound up being caught out of position a few times. Like other Canadian players, he wasn't used to the east-west movement of the Soviets or their strong desire to make so many passes to find the perfect shot. He was at his best when he had the puck and could make his great passes to teammates in the right spot. Park had a strong game in the second contest in Toronto (in Maple Leaf Gardens, which felt like home for him because of his junior days) when he assisted on the first two goals of the game by Phil Esposito and Yvan Cournoyer (the Montreal speedster was sprung into the clear by a brilliant pass from the stick of Park). He wasn't especially prominent in the other games in Canada but he played his best hockey of the series in Moscow.

Park was a very resilient performer for the Canadian side and never let any bad plays or mistakes get him down. It helped that he was teamed with veteran Gary Bergman for most of the series and they complemented each other very well on the ice. He played his finest game in the last contest when he scored a goal and added an assist on another. His goal came late in the first period with Canada down 2–1. He joined the rush led by New York teammate Jean Ratelle and took a pass before beating Tretiak with a well-placed shot. It was an important tally since it sent the teams to the dressing room tied 2–2 and gave Canada a chance to regroup with the score tied after a wild first period.

Park's main contribution to the third-period rally for Team Canada in the final game was his long cross-ice pass to Esposito, which helped to initiate the sequence that led to Cournoyer's goal that tied the game 5–5. His good play throughout the final contest was rewarded with one of the player of the game honours for Canada (the other went to Paul Henderson). All of the five points he earned in the series were crucial and he ended up a plus four with only two penalty minutes — indicating he was able to keep his cool while others around him struggled badly with on-ice discipline.

Park retuned to the Rangers after the series and was excellent for them year after year, but that still didn't stop the New York club from trading him away. He had many good years in Boston (including two more trips to the finals) but couldn't grab the elusive Stanley Cup. He finished his Hall of Fame career with a couple of seasons as a Detroit Red Wing. He recorded 896 points (213G, 683A) in 1,113 career games and was a five-time first-team all-star.

One of the early problems Team Canada encountered in the series was that many of the players were bitter enemies in the NHL. Brad Park had written a book in 1971 in which he was very disparaging to every member of the Boston Bruins who had been selected to Team Canada (except for goalie Eddie Johnston). The Rangers and Bruins were vying for the Stanley Cup every year from 1968 to 1972 with some players really disliking each other. It was a strange sight to see Park and Esposito (someone Park had been especially critical of in his book) hugging after the opening goal of the game in Toronto, but this series clearly broke down some barriers — at least for a short time.

In 1984 when many Edmonton Oiler and New York Islander players found themselves on Team Canada for the Canada Cup tournament, there were many stories about how the two groups of key performers didn't get along. Both teams had been Stanley Cup rivals since 1981. Eventually the team pulled together and won the '84 tournament.

JEAN RATELLE
Career Summary

The New York Rangers were having little success as the 1960s began, but they had a couple of prospects playing on their junior team in Guelph, Ontario, who really had them excited. One was right winger Rod Gilbert and the other was centre Jean Ratelle — both natives of Quebec. Both had also escaped the clutches of the Montreal Canadiens who for years had the first chance to sign promising youngsters from Quebec. Luckily for New York, the Habs couldn't sign up all the good players from that province. Ratelle joined the Guelph Biltmores in time for the 1958–59 season, and over the course of three full seasons with the team, Ratelle would record 238 points (including 99 goals) in just 149 games.

Despite the impressive totals, Ratelle spent the better part of three seasons playing minor league hockey. He was very good in short stints with the Rangers (scoring a goal in his first ever NHL game) starting in 1960–61, but wasn't a full-time member of the team until the 1964–65 campaign when he had 35 points in 54 games for New York. The 1965–66 season saw him score 21 times and register 51 points in 64 games played. Ratelle had to overcome a serious back injury by having spinal-fusion surgery, but he was able to come back in fine form. In 1967–68, he had 78 points in 74 games and he was just short of a point-a-game player for three straight years. Ratelle's game was smooth, skilled, and highly effective at one of the most vital positions in hockey. The Rangers built their team around Ratelle and Gilbert and soon the two were back playing together as they had in junior.

By 1970–71, the Rangers had become serious contenders for the Stanley Cup and made it to the semi-finals that year. A seventh-game loss to Chicago in the semi-finals ended their

Jean Ratelle tries to get the better of the Toronto Maple Leafs' Tim Horton.

hopes but the following season, 1971–72, saw the New York club make it all the way to the final. Ratelle had 46 goals and 109 points (both career highs) in '71–'72, but an ankle injury slowed him down in the playoffs. He was limited to just six games and recorded only one point. If Ratelle had been healthy, the Rangers would have given the Boston Bruins a harder battle in the finals. However, Ratelle's consistent play and his great year earned him a spot on Team Canada for the series versus the Russians. His linemates, Gilbert and Vic Hadfield, also went along for the eight-game ride.

'72 Series Performance

It was a bit of an up-and-down series for Jean Ratelle when Team Canada met the Soviet Union in 1972. Not much went right early on in the series and the Ranger line that started together in Montreal was never together again as a trio. It went a little better for Ratelle when the series shifted to Winnipeg and he scored a pretty goal to give Team Canada a 2–1 lead late in the first period. Even though he had played a very good game, Ratelle still found himself out of the lineup when the series moved to Vancouver (even though Gilbert and Hadfield both dressed) for the fourth contest.

However, Ratelle didn't get down about his status on the team and soon found himself playing in all four games scheduled for Moscow. He was a very steadying influence on the team and did some great work killing penalties. When Hadfield left the team, Dennis Hull of Chicago was placed in his spot and the Black Hawk winger seemed to fit right in with the Rangers' stars. The line scored some very important goals and gave Team Canada another steady trio they could count on for offence or defence. Ratelle assisted on a very important goal by Gilbert in the seventh game and he followed that up with two key assists (one on a goal by Brad Park and the other on a goal by Bill White) in the final game of the series. Ratelle played his usual clean game and was a great example of how sportsmanship could still exist even in the face of some very chaotic hockey!

Ratelle didn't record a single penalty in the six games he played versus the Russians. The only other players not to take a penalty for Canada and appear in at least five games were Frank Mahovlich and Serge Savard. It is interesting to note that Ratelle was the only player on the '72 team to have won the Lady Byng Trophy (given to the player who demonstrated sportsmanship combined with excellent play) prior to the start of the series (three others went on to win it afterward: Gilbert Perreault, Marcel Dionne, and Stan Mikita). Ratelle won the Byng once more before his career ended.

Ratelle put in some more excellent seasons on Broadway (including a 91-point effort in 1974–75), but after 15 years of wearing a Ranger uniform, he was dealt to the Bruins along with Brad Park. To say both New York stars were shocked would be an understatement, but Ratelle still posted 105 points in 1975–76 — the season in which he was traded. He recorded seasons of

94, 84, 72, and 73 over the next four years in Boston. The only thing Ratelle missed during his Hall of Fame career was playing for a Stanley Cup winner. His career totals include 491 goals and 1,267 points.

Jean Ratelle didn't dress for the second game of the series in Toronto, but he came out onto the ice before the game to accept the Lester B. Pearson Trophy from the former Canadian prime minister who was in attendance and wearing his customary bow tie. Ratelle was given the award as the MVP of the NHL for his play in 1971–72 as voted by the players. Other '72 Team Canada players to win the Pearson were Phil Esposito, Bobby Orr, Bobby Clarke, and Marcel Dionne. The trophy has since been renamed the Ted Lindsay Award in honour of the former Detroit Red Wing great who was instrumental in trying to start up the first ever players' association.

RON ELLIS
Career Summary

The Toronto Maple Leafs knew exactly what they were getting when right winger Ron Ellis was going to join the team in time for the 1964–65 season — a player who would be the model of consistency. Ellis had been in the Leaf system since he joined the Toronto Marlboros as a 17-year-old in 1961–62. In his 126-game career as a Marlie, the smooth-skating Ellis recorded 159 points and that included a 46-goal effort in his final year of Junior A. The 1963–64 Marlies featured a great number of players who would go on to play in the NHL (including Peter Stemkowski, Mike Walton, Brit Selby, Wayne Carleton, Jim McKenney, and Brian Glennie), and the Toronto squad easily captured the Memorial Cup.

Ellis was a very good rookie for the Leafs in '64–'65 with 23 goals and 39 points and would have won the Calder Trophy as the top newcomer except for the great season goalie Roger Crozier had in Detroit. His goal production slipped to 19 a year later but in 1966–67, he led the Leafs in goals scored with 22. The '67 playoffs saw the Leafs capture the Stanley Cup and Ellis scored twice in 12 games — the second goal coming in the game that clinched the championship for Toronto. Ellis scored the first marker in the very close sixth game of the finals that ended 3–1 for the Leafs over the favoured Montreal Canadiens. The Leafs slipped back to the status of a team that had to fight every year for the fourth and final playoff spot but Ellis's game never wavered. He scored 28, 25, 35, 24, and 23 goals over the next five years and was a solid defensive forward every season.

Ellis was a smart hockey player and could read the play easily. He was so defensively responsible (he had been well trained by Punch Imlach, the first coach he had with the Leafs) that he didn't attack as often as possible. He had great speed and could break in off the wing when he was given a pass in full stride. His goal-scoring touch was very good, not great, but in 1969–70,

Toronto Maple Leaf Ron Ellis (8) looks on with teammate Frank Mahovlich as Detroit players, including Paul Henderson (19), storm Leafs goaltender Terry Sawchuk.

he scored a career-best 35 goals and it looked as if he might have broken through to a new level. No matter what Ellis did on offence, he was still one of the best defensive forwards in hockey. He was often assigned to check the likes of Chicago's Bobby Hull and, after he was traded from the Leafs to Detroit, Frank Mahovlich. Ellis would never give a goal away without a fight and he often outplayed the man he was shadowing.

Left winger Paul Henderson and centre Norm Ullman became Ellis's linemates in Toronto and the trio was known as the "HUE" line. Ullman wasn't considered for Team Canada in 1972, but when 38-goal scorer Henderson was selected, it made sense to invite his linemate on the right side as well. It turned out to be a very good move to have Ellis on the '72 team.

'72 Series Performance

Ron Ellis didn't score a single goal during the entire eight-game series versus the Russians, but he was still one of the better players on the team. The line of Ellis, Henderson, and Bobby Clarke stayed together the whole series and their play was very consistent if not outstanding. While Ellis was held off the scoreboard, he did help to create a great deal of offence (recording three assists), and he had some outstanding chances to score on Vladislav Tretiak, but the Russian goalie had his number and stopped every Ellis drive on net. Ellis had a very hard and heavy shot but it couldn't find a way past Tretiak.

In predictable fashion, as soon as Team Canada realized that Valery Kharlamov was the best Russian threat to score, Ellis was immediately assigned to check the slick winger. Kharlamov scored twice in the opening game and once more in Winnipeg but never hit the back of the Canadian net again (of course it helped that the Soviet player missed a game and wasn't his usual self after a Clarke stick attack). Ellis's hardest shot on goal came on a play in the seventh contest that was ruled offside. The drive made Tretiak jump and struck him high. The goalie was clearly shaken up but he didn't leave the game. Ellis was very physical throughout the entire series and never made it easy for the Russians to enter the Canadian end of the ice.

If there was an enduring image of Ellis in the series, it came late in the sixth game with Canada up 3–2. He was whistled off for holding on a very marginal call by the referee. Ellis proceeded to sweat for the entire two-minute minor, pounding his leg with his fist, praying the Russians wouldn't score. Ellis's teammates killed off the penalty and Canada was still alive to win the series. If the Russians had scored, the very serious-minded Ellis would never have forgiven himself.

Upon his return to the NHL, the now-veteran winger was once again a productive scorer, notching 32 goals in 1974–75. He abruptly quit hockey for a couple of seasons but then returned to score 26 times in 1977–78 — a year that saw the Leafs win their first seven-game playoff series since 1967! Ellis played two more years before his 1,034-game career (all with the Maple Leafs) ended. He finished with 332 goals and 640 points.

Canada sent a group of players from teams that missed the Stanley Cup playoffs or bowed out in the early rounds to the 1977 World Hockey Championships. Ron Ellis didn't play in the NHL during the 1976–77 season, but was recruited to play for the Canadian team. There he scored five goals and accumulated nine points in 10 games played. Also on the roster were three other members of the 1972 Team Canada: Phil Esposito, Rod Gilbert, and Tony Esposito. The team, coached by Johnny Wilson, finished a miserable fourth and out of the medals but at least Canada was back in the tournament.

BRIAN GLENNIE
Career Summary

For many years, hockey players ignored their education to focus solely on hockey, but Toronto Maple Leaf defenceman Brian Glennie was an exception. He pursued his education at the University of Toronto (where he was earning a degree in physical education) while he was playing junior hockey for the Toronto Marlboros. Glennie's junior career was highlighted by a Memorial Cup win in 1967 when the powerful Marlies (a team he captained) beat out all the competition for the coveted trophy. Glennie was named the most valuable player of the talented team, recording 25 points in 26 post-season games. It was expected he would immediately try for a position on the Leafs blueline since many of the old rearguards (like Tim Horton, Marcel Pronovost, and Allan Stanley) were moving out or getting older. However, the 1967–68 season saw Glennie play for the Canadian National Team, which competed for the country at the 1968 Winter Olympics in Grenoble, France. The Canadian team won the bronze medal with Glennie recording one point in seven games.

During the 1968–69 season Glennie underwent surgery on one shoulder and then he played in the minors for two Leaf farm teams — the Rochester Americans and the Tulsa Oilers. He was very impressive with the Oilers in the playoffs with four points in seven games. By the time the 1969–70 season rolled around, the 23-year-old Glennie was a Leaf defenceman for 52 games (recording 15 points) and was on his way to establishing his NHL career. He played in 54 games the following year (no goals, eight assists), and helped the Maple Leafs get back into the playoffs. The 1971–72 season had Glennie participating in 61 games (2G, 8A), and he was improving his play each time out. He was quickly gaining a reputation for his devastating bodychecks delivered right in the middle of the ice. "Glennie hits like a truck" was a popular sign at Maple Leaf Gardens as the Toronto fans came to appreciate the low-scoring but very rugged defenceman.

The 1972 playoffs had the Maple Leafs playing the Boston

Toronto Maple Leaf Brian Glennie sails behind the net, with a Los Angeles Kings player in close pursuit.

Bruins in the first round and Glennie made life miserable for forwards like Phil Esposito and Ken Hodge. The bruising Leaf blueliner was solid at six feet, one inch and 197 pounds, but he always made sure he was in top condition. He wasn't fast on his skates but he learned to position himself properly to make the most of his physical skills. While he might have been an unlikely selection for Team Canada in 1972, he did have international experience and there was obviously a need to have Maple Leaf players on the team to help create interest. The Toronto native was honoured to be a part of Team Canada.

'72 Series Performance

If the early part of the series had gone better for Team Canada, Brian Glennie might have been able to get in some games but when the Russians won the opener 7–3, it meant that some players weren't going to get a chance. It was especially difficult for coaches like Harry Sinden and John Ferguson to consider a defenceman like Glennie who might have had a very difficult time against the smaller, speedier Soviet players. Team Canada settled down back of the blueline when players like Rod Seiling and Don Awrey (defencemen similar in style to Glennie) were dropped from the lineup and six steady blueliners finished out the last three games of the series.

Glennie's only two appearances in the Team Canada uniform came in Sweden and Czechoslovakia. The Canadians took the Swedish game with a 4–1 score and it was interesting to note that two future Maple Leafs played in that contest. One was defenceman Borje Salming and the other was forward Inge Hammarstrom. Neither player was signed by the Leafs at that point but both would join Glennie on the Leaf team for the 1973–74 season. The game in Czechoslovakia saw Canada get a last-minute goal to secure a 3–3 tie. Glennie didn't register a point or any penalties in either game.

It must have been tempting for Glennie (and others) to leave the team once he knew there was no chance of playing in Moscow, but he stayed for the duration of the series. Glennie certainly wanted to provide support for his Toronto teammates, Ron Ellis and Paul Henderson. In fact, Henderson recalled that Glennie gave him a big bear hug in the dressing room after the final game when he had scored the winning goal!

When Team Canada came home on the night of October 1, 1972, they were greeted by an emotional but happy crowd of fans. Thousands of people (estimated at somewhere between 30,000 and 40,000) had braved a very rainy night to salute the team at Toronto's city hall. Glennie made the mood even lighter by asking if anyone had a cheeseburger on hand since he was so tired of eating very bad Russian food! In an interview about a year later during the Canadian National Exhibition, Glennie told the assembled outdoor crowd he kissed the ground when he arrived back home in Canada after what he had seen and experienced in the Soviet Union.

Glennie was a Maple Leaf for six more seasons and played some of his best hockey in the 1978 playoffs when Toronto eliminated the Los Angeles Kings in a best-of-three series and then the New York Islanders in a best-of-seven that went the distance. In the summer of 1978, Glennie was traded to the Kings but a bad back effectively ended his career after only 18 games in a Los Angeles uniform. He retired after 572 career games, recording 114 points and 621 penalty minutes.

> Great nicknames have always been a part of hockey and no player had a better handle to describe his style of play than Brian Glennie who was simply called "Blunt." Glennie's Maple Leaf and '72 Team Canada teammate Ron Ellis was called "Chevy" for his resemblance to Canadian heavyweight boxer George Chuvalo. Other notable nicknames for '72 Team Canada members include "Big M" (for Frank Mahovlich), "Red Baron" (for Gordon Berenson), "Whitey" (for Pat Stapleton), and "Little Beaver" (for Marcel Dionne).

MICKEY REDMOND
Career Summary

If there was one thing right winger Mickey Redmond could do it was score goals — lots of them. The native of Kirkland Lake, Ontario, was developed in the Montreal Canadiens organization and was a top scorer for the Peterborough Petes of the OHA for four seasons starting when he was just 16 years old. In 201 games for the Peterborough club, Redmond scored 136 goals. That total included a 51-goal season in 1966–67, which saw him named the most valuable player in the entire league (he had 95 points during a 48-game regular season). The Montreal club was still loaded with quality veterans who had won Stanley Cups and that meant the five-foot, 11-inch, 185-pound Redmond had to start the 1967–68 season in the minors. There he had 17 points in 19 games, which got him promoted to the Habs for 41 games during the same year. With limited ice time, Redmond managed six goals and 11 points and was with the club when they won the Stanley Cup in the '68 playoffs.

Redmond was a full-time NHL player for the 1968–69 season and he appeared in 65 games while getting his point total up to 24. He made a more significant contribution in the '69 playoffs by scoring the winning goal in overtime versus Boston and had five points in 14 post-season contests. His name was on the Stanley Cup for a second time and he had only played in two seasons!

Redmond's game was built around his ability to appear at just the right moment to rap a puck into the net. Even though he was an excellent skater, Redmond didn't carry the puck much, but when he let his excellent shot go, it often found the back of the opposition net. In 1969–70, Redmond scored 27 times and added 27 assists, but for one of the rare times in their history to that point, the Canadiens missed the playoffs in the tough East Division of the NHL.

Montreal still had many good players on their team and in the minor system, and they could go after a great player by using this wealth of depth. When Frank Mahovlich was made available, the Habs packaged Redmond and two other players to the Detroit Red Wings for the long-time

Mickey Redmond's Team Canada '72
playing card — he won two Stanley Cups
with the Montreal Canadiens, then was
traded to the Detroit Red Wings in the deal
that brought Frank Mahovlich to the Habs.

(Future Trends Experience Ltd.)

star. Redmond wasn't happy to leave Montreal but soon realized that he would get a chance to play in Detroit that he wouldn't likely get as a Canadien. He was traded in the middle of the 1970–71 season, and although Detroit was a very bad team at the time, Redmond managed to score 20 goals in total (14 came as a Hab in the first 40 games of the season). Redmond played alongside veteran centre Alex Delvecchio in Detroit and scored 42 goals (the ninth-best league mark) in the 1971–72 season. He scored 32 goals at even strength and the other 10 on the power play while taking 271 shots on net. Team Canada selectors wanted Redmond's offensive flair on the right side and gave him a spot on the team.

'72 Series Performance

Mickey Redmond was in the opening night lineup at the Montreal Forum where he had enjoyed many good games. However, this would be the only game Redmond would get to play in. He was good on the attack, directing four shots at the net and making Tretiak stop another. The Russians scored one of their goals while he was on the ice but he didn't see a great deal of playing time.

Redmond might have been more effective had he received more of an opportunity but a bad back (and/or a viral infection) seemed to make that impossible. He wasn't as gritty as some of the other wingers on the team (like J.P. Parise or Wayne Cashman) but he was more talented and could have come in handy on the attack. He went with the team to Moscow but could only be a cheerleader for the Canadian side. He wasn't able to dress for any of the other games in Europe but he did sit with the team at the end of the bench for at least one of the Moscow games while wearing his overcoat.

However, the preparation for the series did Redmond a world of good for the 1972–73 season because he became the first Red Wing to score 50 goals in one season (Gordie Howe never scored more than 49) when he finished the campaign with 52. To prove that was no fluke he scored 51 the following season, but the Red Wings were still a very poor team despite Redmond's impressive performance. His goal-scoring prowess came along at just the right time to earn him a $1 million, five-year contract from the Red Wings who didn't want to lose him to the World Hockey Association.

A serious back injury forced a premature end to a shining career at the tender age of 28. His final totals are still very impressive (428 points in 538 career games) and his 233-goal tally would have been much higher had he played well past the age of 30. His brother Dick was an NHL defenceman for 13 seasons spent with six different teams.

> Many hockey players try their hand at broadcasting once their playing careers are over and Mickey Redmond has done very well in this field as a game analyst. He was on *Hockey Night in Canada* for a while but has made his mark on the local broadcasts of the Detroit Red Wing games. He has been fortunate enough to see the Red Wings win the Stanley Cup in 1997, 1998, 2002, and 2008.

RICK MARTIN
Career Summary

When left winger Rick Martin was 13 years of age he played two levels of hockey — bantam and midget. He finished in the top 10 of goal scorers in both divisions. The native of Verdun, Quebec, scored 85 goals for his bantam team and added another 30 for his midget squad. Part of the reason for Martin's great success was that he practised his shot repeatedly. He admired Bobby Hull as a youngster and the Chicago superstar scored many of his goals by using his overpowering slap shot. Martin never really used a big windup like Hull did but he could get almost as much power into his hard drives, which scared more than one goalie he faced growing up. He liked to shoot the puck and was very accurate with his drives, making goaltenders feel the hard rubber even if he didn't score.

Martin was 16 when he played for Thetford in the QJHL and scored 38 times in just 40 games and that got him to the Montreal Jr. Canadiens for the 1968–69 season. In three seasons played for the OHA club, Martin continued his prolific goal scoring with 116 goals in 146 games. He also produced at more than a point-a-game pace and won two consecutive Memorial Cups in 1969 and 1970 — one of the few times the Canadian junior championship has been won by the same team in consecutive years. Many of the players on the Jr. Canadiens made it to the NHL. His most famous teammate with the Jr. Canadiens was Gilbert Perreault who would also be his teammate with the Buffalo Sabres and with Team Canada in 1972.

Martin's final year of junior saw him score 71 times in 60 games, while amassing 121 points. Such a great performance had him ranked high up for the 1971 NHL Entry Draft and he was selected fifth overall by the Buffalo Sabres. He was pleased to head to western New York since his great friend Perreault had enjoyed a very successful rookie year in Buffalo in 1970–71 and he felt he would be treated very well there. Sabres general manager George "Punch" Imlach was thrilled to add Martin to his new team (the Sabres had just completed their first ever NHL season) and realized his left wing recruit was a pure shooter — the type of player every team needs if they are going to compete offensively.

Perreault had set an NHL rookie record with 38 goals and all Martin did in his first year was break that mark with 44 tallies (Martin's total was later surpassed). The Sabres weren't a good team yet, but they were off to a great start with the two youngsters they had drafted in their first two seasons. Martin would have won the rookie of the year award but the Calder Trophy went to goalie Ken Dryden who enjoyed the advantage of playing 20 playoff games in the 1971 post-season. Even though he was just 21, Team Canada invited the youngster to its training camp in September 1972. It was hoped they could use him alongside Perreault, but that never material-ized during the Summit Series (though the match-up did come together for the two Sabre stars in the 1976 Canada Cup).

'72 Series Performance

When the '72 series became a furious battle, there was little room for experimentation or younger, inexperienced players. Martin didn't play in any games in Canada but did travel with the team over to Europe. Martin played one game against Sweden and promptly scored a goal during a 4–4 tie (with the lone assist going to Perreault). Once it was apparent that there was no chance of him playing in any of the Moscow games, Martin decided he would be better served by going home and preparing for the NHL season. Young and perhaps a little too cocky, Martin may have acted a little impulsively and left Team Canada quickly once they arrived in Moscow. His good friend Perreault joined him just one day later even though he had played in the fifth game of the series. Four players left the team in Moscow but it has never been held against any of them at any reunions of the '72 team or for any project that involved the team as a whole. Everyone was welcomed to the events organized for the team especially the always-ready-with-a-quip Martin.

Martin had 73 points in 75 games during the 1972–73 season so his early training camp work certainly paid off for the young star. He would score 52 goals in each of the next two seasons and was a consistent star for the Sabres for a number of years. The Buffalo squad was in the Stanley Cup final in 1975 and was expected to win it all but they always fell a little short between 1976 and 1980. Martin suffered a bad knee injury in November 1980 and that led to his being traded to the Los Angeles Kings. He was only able to play in four games for the Kings (scoring two goals) before he was forced to retire at the age of 30. He finished with 384 goals and 701 points in just 635 career games and was a four-time league all-star. The numbers suggest he would have been considered a Hall of Fame candidate if he had been able to play longer.

On March 13, 2011, the hockey world was saddened to learn that Rick Martin died of a heart attack while driving a car at the age of 57. He became the fourth member of the 1972 Team Canada roster to pass away. The first was Bill Goldsworthy (in 1996) and then defenceman Gary Bergman (in 2000). Assistant coach John Ferguson passed away in 2007.

EDDIE JOHNSTON
Career Summary

The Boston Bruins made it to the Stanley Cup finals in both 1958 and 1959 only to lose each time to the Montreal Canadiens who were in the middle of winning five straight championships. After that time, a number of Bruin veterans were fading and were moved off the team, but Boston's biggest problem was that it lacked a quality goalie. The Bruins tried such journeymen as Bruce Gamble, Don Head, Jack Norris, and Bobby Perreault but none of them could do the job required. However, Eddie Johnston, a native of Montreal, soon caught the eye of Bruins management and they decided to select the young netminder from Chicago's list in the intraleague draft of 1962. The new goalie didn't solve all of Boston's problems but at least they had someone who could give them respectable goaltending most nights.

Johnston was already 27 years old by the time he played 50 games for the Bruins in the 1962–63 season. He had enjoyed some good years in the minors and had won a slew of awards when he played in the EPHL for the Ottawa-Hull team during the 1960–61 season, a campaign that saw him win 41 times in 70 games played during the regular season. He won another eight in the playoffs. He was with Spokane in 1961–62 and won 37 games for the team in the Western Hockey League. The Bruins decided to give him a chance in the big league and he won 11 games as a rookie behind a very poor team. It wasn't unusual for a goalie to play in the minors for some years in the "Golden Era," when NHL teams only employed one goalie. Even though he lost 27 times in his first season, it was evident Johnston's days in the minors were over.

Outside of the 1963–64 season, Johnston always shared the Boston net with another goalie. Bernie Parent joined the team in 1964–65 and later on Gerry Cheevers was added to the team after he was picked up from Toronto. The Bruins were definitely improved in net but they didn't make the playoffs until coach Harry Sinden joined the team along with superstars Bobby Orr and Phil Esposito.

Parent was lost in the 1967 expansion draft with the Bruins believing Cheevers and Johnston would take them far into the playoffs. By 1968, the Boston club had at long last become a contender and by the spring of 1970, they were Stanley Cup champions. Johnston enjoyed a 16-win season in '69–'70 and won 30 times in 1970–71, a career best for the six-foot, 190-pound goalie. The year was ruined when Montreal upset the Bruins in the '71 playoffs but the next season saw the Bruins recapture the Stanley Cup. Johnston played in seven post-season games in 1972 and won six of those starts with a 1.86 goals-against-average. He was in net the night the Bruins

Boston Bruins goaltender Eddie Johnston tries to finesse the Toronto Maple Leafs' Ron Ellis.

nearly won the Cup on home ice, but the New York Rangers spoiled the party by winning a close game 3–2. It was the fifth game of the finals and the Boston team badly wanted to win it in front of their fans but it wasn't meant to be in that contest. Cheevers was back in goal the next game when the Bruins clinched the Cup in New York.

When Cheevers decided to leave Boston for the large dollars offered by the new professional league (the World Hockey Association), he was ruled as unavailable for the '72 Summit Series. Coach Harry Sinden turned to the 36-year-old Johnston, since he knew he could rely on the steady netminder to be insurance if Ken Dryden or Tony Esposito were injured.

'72 Series Performance

It became clear very early that Eddie Johnston wasn't going to get into any of the eight games versus the Russians. Sinden had decided that Dryden and Esposito were going to rotate starts and that was how it went for the most part. Johnston was in uniform for six of the eight games (missing only the first and last contests) but he was strictly the backup and never saw a minute of action against the Russians. The closest he came to getting into a game was in Moscow when Esposito was badly stung when he took a high shot to the neck area. However, Esposito was able to recover and finished the seventh game.

Johnston did play the entire game against Sweden in the second of two contests against the Swedish national team and played very well despite giving up four goals in a 4–4 draw. He faced 31 shots in the contest and many were of the difficult variety, with Canada taking far too many penalties in the tune-up game. If nothing else, Johnston showed that he was ready to contribute if called upon. Johnston had never complained about not being a number one goalie and he wasn't about to start by expressing concern about his status on Team Canada.

Johnston had a very good year in 1972–73, posting a 24–17–1 record. Nevertheless, he was traded to the Toronto Maple Leafs prior to the start of the next season. He gave the Leafs some veteran stability in the 26 games he appeared in but was on the move again — this time to St. Louis. He played in the NHL until the age of 42 and won 234 games, 32 of them shutouts, and two championships — a very good record considering Johnston was in the minors for seven seasons before he got his chance!

Eddie Johnston was the last NHL netminder to play a complete season for his team. He played in all 70 games during the 1963–64 season, posting an 18–40–12 mark with six shutouts. Ken Dryden never played more than 64 games in any one season for Montreal while Tony Esposito played in 71 games for Chicago in 1974–75, a season that featured an 80-game schedule.

DALE TALLON
Career Summary

Dale Tallon was compared to somebody else for pretty much his entire playing career. It started in junior hockey when he was with the Oshawa Generals — a team that had seen the great Bobby Orr graduate to the NHL just two years earlier. Tallon had 43 points in 50 games for the Generals in 1967–68, but the team felt he was under too much pressure being compared to Orr so they decided to trade him to the Toronto Marlboros in exchange for five players. If it was a deal that was supposed to relieve some pressure, imagine how he felt trying to make up the value of five players! However, Tallon put all negative thoughts aside and had two great years in Toronto while playing every forward position and defence. He scored 39 goals and added 40 assists in 54 games for the Marlies during his last junior season in 1969–70. He added 29 points in 18 playoff games and all the talk was that he was considered one of the most promising youngsters available in the 1970 NHL Entry Draft.

The problem for Tallon was that he was now being compared with centre Gilbert Perreault who was considered the best junior in all of Canada. Perreault and the Montreal Jr. Canadiens had defeated Tallon and the Marlies for the OHA title in the 1970 playoffs, and the two rivals were clearly the best players on the ice. The Buffalo Sabres and the Vancouver Canucks were set to join the NHL for the 1970–71 season and they would select the first two players at the draft. The Sabres won the right to pick first and took Perreault and that meant Tallon, a native of Noranda, Quebec, would head to the West Coast of Canada. The six-foot, one-inch, 195-pound Tallon wanted to establish himself as a defenceman, but more than one person in the Canucks organization thought he should play at forward. Perreault had no such concerns about what position he was going to play.

Further pressure fell upon Tallon's shoulders when his salary was leaked out (an estimated $60,000 a year for two seasons it was reported in some places) and that made some veteran players upset that a rookie was getting so much money. Tallon struggled in training camp and was shifted around to different positions but still managed to score 14 goals and total 56 points for an expansion team. Both Buffalo and Vancouver won 24 games in 1970–71, but Perreault was the best rookie with 38 goals, a then record for first-year players. The next season saw Tallon spend time on defence (the position he most preferred) and the wing. He scored 17 times but his point total dropped to 44 and a late-season injury to his knee cut his game total to 69.

The Canucks only really had the 21-year-old Tallon and defenceman Jocelyn Guevremont as rising talents and they were included on Team Canada in 1972 because it was deemed necessary that the Vancouver team was represented. It turned out their participation was mostly for show.

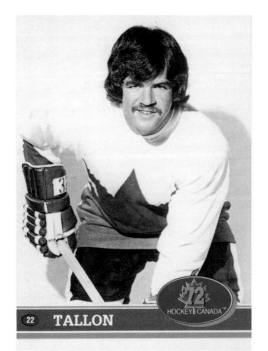

Dale Tallon's Team Canada '72 playing card. Plagued with injuries during his short career, he ended up playing for the Vancouver Canucks, the Chicago Black Hawks, and the Pittsburgh Penguins.

[Future Trends Experience Ltd.]

'72 Series Performance

Dale Tallon didn't dress for any of Team Canada's games against the Soviets. However, it was noteworthy when broadcaster Foster Hewitt said early in the television broadcast of the final game from Moscow that Tallon was ready to play if defenceman Pat Stapleton, who was nursing a leg injury, was unable to go. It says something about Tallon's talent that the coaches were willing to put him into the lineup of such an important game without having played the Russians in the previous seven games.

Tallon did play one game against Sweden and he was aggressive all night long. He took one slashing and one roughing penalty in the game but contributed an assist when Phil Esposito scored in the last minute to secure a 4–4 tie. Tallon played an emotionally charged game on a Canadian team that showed a great disdain for all the players on the Swedish team. Tallon was also in the lineup when Team Canada played a final game in Czechoslovakia and he was penalized for high sticking. The game was another tie for the young defenceman; this time the final score was 3–3.

Tallon played well for Vancouver in 1972–73 (13 goals) but the team wasn't improving very much. The Canucks decided to move Tallon to the Chicago Black Hawks in return for Jerry Korab and goalie Gary Smith. Tallon would never be spectacular over the remaining seven seasons in the NHL (five with Chicago, two with Pittsburgh) before he retired. He had 336 points in 642 career games, but his real mark would be made in his role as an NHL executive.

After years spent in broadcasting, Tallon was named the general manager of the Blackhawks (the Black Hawks were renamed in 1986), where he did a great job in reshaping the team through excellent drafting, trading, and signing of free agents. In 2010, the Chicago team won the Stanley Cup for the first time since 1961, largely through the efforts of Tallon. He wasn't the general manager of record (he had been replaced in that role by Stan Bowman), but it was essentially his team that won it all. Finally, Tallon had escaped all the comparisons about who was the best. He was named general manager of the Florida Panthers for the 2011–12 season.

The Florida Panthers had missed the playoffs for 10 seasons until Dale Tallon took over the team for the 2011–12 campaign. Tallon used veterans and youngsters to make the Panthers something of a contender in just one season. Rookie coach Kevin Dineen also helped steer the Panthers into the post-season in 2012. Tallon is the only member of the '72 Team Canada roster in an active managerial role in 2012.

BILL GOLDSWORTHY
Career Summary

Right winger Bill Goldsworthy was recruited by the Boston Bruins and played his junior hockey with the Niagara Falls Flyers of the Ontario Hockey League. The Flyers had strong teams and Goldsworthy played in the Memorial Cup playoffs twice — on the losing end in 1963 and on the winning side in 1965. The '65 Flyers had many players on the team that went on to play for the Bruins and other NHL teams, including Bernie Parent, Derek Sanderson, Don Marcotte, Jean Pronovost, Rick Ley, and Doug Favell. Goldsworthy scored 28 goals in 54 regular season games and then added another 16 during the march to the championship. Goldsworthy was called up for two games in Boston during the 1964–65 season, but found himself in the minors at the start of his professional career.

The Bruins were trying to sort out all their prospects and had many good players down in Oklahoma City with their farm club but Goldsworthy didn't put up impressive numbers over two Central Professional Hockey League seasons. The six-foot, one-inch, 190-pound Goldsworthy was better when he was assigned to Buffalo in the AHL, recording 20 points in 22 games. He scored six goals in 31 games for the Bruins when they gave him a look, but they didn't like him enough to protect him in the 1967 expansion draft held in June of that year. Wren Blair, who was very familiar with the Boston system, liked what he saw of Goldsworthy enough to select him for the team he was now managing — the Minnesota North Stars. Goldsworthy was glad to go to an expansion team where he knew he would get a better chance to play and stay in the NHL. He hated being shuffled between the minors and the big league, which caused him to be undisciplined at times.

Goldsworthy still had trouble getting going but did manage to score 14 times for the North Stars in 1967–68. However, he was a star in the '68 playoffs when he scored eight goals and had 15 points in 14 post-season games. Blair hoped his good playoff would lead to a more productive

The Minnesota North Stars' Bill Goldsworthy (8) races for the puck while fighting off Toronto's feisty Ian Turnbull. (Graphic Artists/Hockey Hall of Fame)

year in 1968–69, but Goldsworthy was still not all he could be and once again finished with just 14 tallies and 24 points. He was even back in the minors for a short stint. But in 1969–70, the hard-shooting winger suddenly found his game, scoring 36 times (the sixth highest total in the league) and recording 65 points in 75 games. "Goldy" had finally arrived.

The next two seasons were very good ones for Goldsworthy with 34 goals in 1970–71 and 31 for the 1971–72 campaign. The North Stars briefly challenged for the Stanley Cup in 1971 before they were beaten by the Montreal Canadiens. The '72 post-season saw them lose to St. Louis but Goldsworthy had proven himself a top goal scorer and a player who could be counted upon to score 60 or more points. Team Canada coach Harry Sinden knew what fun-loving Goldsworthy could do if he was in the right frame of mind and invited him to join the team. It was also hoped he might play with Jean-Paul Parise, a left winger on the North Stars who was a good corner man.

'72 Series Performance

Bill Goldsworthy played in three games versus the Russians and his play was memorable, although too often for the wrong reasons. Sinden took some of the blame for telling Goldsworthy to be aggressive but the North Star took it to an extreme in his limited time on the ice. Goldsworthy was determined to attack anything in a Russian uniform and was fortunate not to be called for penalties in the Toronto game. He wasn't so lucky in the Vancouver contest and put Team Canada in a deep hole when the Soviets scored twice with Goldsworthy in the penalty box with the needless infractions of cross-checking and elbowing. The Russians used their two-goal lead to cruise to a 5–3 victory. In the third period of the game, Goldsworthy showed why he had been selected with a nice goal and an assist but it was far too late to make up for the way he had started the game.

When the team played in Sweden for two games, Goldsworthy was in the lineup for the second contest and was given a cross-checking minor, a spearing major, and a 10-minute misconduct. Despite his performance against Sweden, Goldsworthy was back in the lineup for the fifth game of the Soviet series in Moscow and he was much better behaved, but he was never far from crossing the line. Goldsworthy wore a helmet in Canada (he was recovering from a concussion suffered in NHL play) but took it off for his only appearance in Moscow.

Goldsworthy's aggressive play was surprising since he didn't often play that way in the NHL (although he did record 110 penalty minutes for the North Stars in 1968–69), especially after Minnesota teammates like Parise had urged him to tone down the retaliation penalties. In 1972–73 Goldsworthy scored 27 times but the next year saw him score 48 — his career-best mark. He was a North Star for two more seasons before they sent him to the New York Rangers to close out his 771-NHL-game career. He finished with 283 goals and 541 points in the NHL before going to the WHA for two more years.

As unpredictable as Bill Goldsworthy may have been on and off the ice, he was the first franchise star for the Minnesota club and was named team captain of the North Stars for two seasons starting in 1974-75. Many other members of Team Canada were named team captains for at least one full season, including Red Berenson, Wayne Cashman, Bobby Clarke, Yvan Cournoyer, Marcel Dionne, Phil Esposito, Vic Hadfield, Stan Mikita, J.P. Parise, Brad Park, Gilbert Perreault, Serge Savard, and Pat Stapleton. Gary Bergman and Mickey Redmond served as captains on the Red Wings, but for only part of the 1973-74 season when Detroit listed seven different players in the capacity.

DENNIS HULL
Career Summary

Dennis Hull idolized his oldest sibling so much that it drove him to be a hockey player. However, being the younger brother of the talented and flamboyant Bobby Hull was no easy task while growing up or as an NHL player. Bobby was hockey's most recognizable super-star. He lifted hockey fans out of their seats wherever he played. Dennis was just 14 years old when his brother broke into the NHL in 1957-58 but he followed in Bobby's footsteps by playing junior hockey in St. Catharines, Ontario. Dennis wasn't the prolific goal scorer that Bobby was early on but by his final season of junior in 1963-64, he scored 48 times in 55 games. The five-foot, 11-inch, 197-pound left winger was starting to get noticed for his size, strength, and heavy shot but still needed to work on his all-round game (especially his skating) if he was going to make it in the big league. Being on the same team as his famous brother didn't help Dennis initially but eventually he carved out his own niche and became a very good player.

Hull spent the 1964-65 season in Chicago but only played in 55 games, while scoring 10 goals. Chicago decided he needed more ice time and sent him to St. Louis of the CPHL for most of the 1965-66 campaign and it paid off with him recording 27 points in 40 games. He was with the Black Hawks for 25 games in '65-'66 but only scored one goal. After training camp for the 1966-67 season was over, Chicago coach Billy Reay told Hull he had made the team and that seemed to give the 22-year-old a boost of confidence. He scored 25 times in his first full season and his minor league days were now behind him. The fans in Chicago weren't easy on Hull, thinking he should be as good as his brother for some reason. However, they soon accepted him for his own skills and he would be a Black Hawk for 12 seasons.

Hull's goal production was up and down for the next three seasons (18, 30, and 17), but in 1970-71 he had a breakthrough season with 40 tallies in 78 regular season games. He scored another seven times in the '71 post-season and the Chicago club came within one game of winning the Stanley Cup. Hull had another good season in 1971-72 (30G, 39A), but the Black Hawks were out of the playoffs early in '72.

Dennis Hull, with Toronto's Tim Horton right behind him,
attempts to outsmart goalie Johnny Bower.

Dennis Hull wasn't expecting an invite to Team Canada in 1972 but, when Bobby was banned because he had signed a deal with the rival World Hockey Association, it was believed Dennis received his invitation as an effort by the NHL to make up for what they had done to his brother. He was going to reject the opportunity but Bobby talked him into going and it gave Dennis a chance to shine without having to be in the shadow of the "Golden Jet." It turned out to be a great move for the younger Hull.

'72 Series Performance

Dennis Hull didn't get into the '72 series until the fourth game in Vancouver. Considering he was very rusty, Hull played a pretty good game and scored a goal very late in the 5–3 loss. Hull had shown he was ready to contribute but was still out of the lineup for the first game in Moscow. He was back in for the sixth game and scored a very important goal just after Canada had fallen

Brothers Dennis and Bobby Hull share a moment in the mid-1960s when they both played for the Chicago Black Hawks.

behind 1–0. Hull was placed on a line with two New York Ranger players, Rod Gilbert and Jean Ratelle, and he seemed to fit in perfectly on the left side. His goal came off a scramble in front of the Soviet goal with Hull swooping in to drive a high shot past Vladislav Tretiak. Hull's goal seemed to change the momentum of the game and Canada scored three quick goals in less than two minutes and then hung on to win the game 3–2. The Canadian side was back in the series.

The line Hull was assigned to stayed together the rest of the series and he picked up two assists (one in each of the remaining two games) to help Canada win the series. Hull was effective throughout and was physical when he had to be against the quick Russian wingers. Hull finished with four points in four games, taking 10 shots on net and was a plus four. Brother Bobby was very proud!

Hull had his best NHL season in 1972–73 when he scored 39 goals and amassed 90 points. He was named to the NHL's second all-star team — the only all-star berth of his career. Chicago was back in the Stanley Cup final in '73 but once again, it was the Montreal Canadiens who walked away with the big silver trophy. Hull put in more fine seasons with the Black Hawks but the team was never as good again. Hull played one last season for the Detroit Red Wings in 1977–78 and his five goals that year gave him a career total of 333 to go along with 654 points in 959 games played — quite a performance for someone who was just thought to be Bobby Hull's brother!

When Dennis Hull returned to Chicago for the 1972–73 season after his '72 Team Canada experience, the line he played on with Jim Pappin and Pit Martin combined to score 109 goals during the 78-game regular season. Hull had 39 goals, Pappin scored 41, and Martin chipped in with 29 for the Black Hawks. The trio also combined for 27 goals in 16 playoff games that saw Chicago go all the way to the final.

WAYNE CASHMAN
Career Summary

When the Boston Bruins acquired Phil Esposito and Ken Hodge from the Chicago Black Hawks prior to the start of the 1967–68 season, they needed to find a left winger to go beside the pair. Veteran Ron Murphy was tried at first but he was soon gone from the team while youngster Ross Lonsberry got hurt. The Bruins also tried star Johnny Bucyk on that line but he was better suited elsewhere. Finally, coach Harry Sinden gave tough, raw-boned Wayne Cashman a shot and suddenly one of the most effective lines in NHL history was born. The six-foot, one-inch, 208-pound Cashman was a right-handed shot so putting him on the left side went against the natural order of how things should work, but the winger found a way to cope with the change. He soon became a major force on a team on the way to a pair of Stanley Cup championships.

Cashman had been in the Bruins organization since his junior days with the Oshawa Generals beginning in 1963–64. He wasn't a great goal scorer nor was he especially skilled, but he was very willing and produced 165 points in 131 games. He spent part of his time with the Generals playing alongside the great Bobby Orr and nearly won a Memorial Cup but lost out to the Edmonton Oil Kings in the final. Cashman was too raw to be considered ready for the NHL after he finished his junior career so he was sent to the Oklahoma City Blazers of the CPHL for two years. He then spent one year with the Hershey Bears of the AHL. The Bruins had long been pushed around during their floundering years between 1960 and 1967 and were hopeful the always aggressive Cashman could give them the rough edge they needed. He scored eight goals in 51 games for Boston in 1968–69. In 1969–70 he played in 70 games and registered 35 points in the team's first championship season.

In 1970–71 Cashman and his linemates combined for 336 points (Esposito had 152), with the bruising winger contributing 79 of them, including 21 goals. The season also marked the first of four straight times that Cashman would record over 100 penalty minutes. The Bruins were upset by Montreal in the 1971 post-season but were ready to reclaim the Cup after the

Wayne Cashman (right) and a very young Bobby Orr
hurtle behind the net in their Oshawa Generals Junior A days.

1971–72 regular season was over. Cashman scored 23 times during that year and then scored two goals in the game that saw Boston clinch their second Stanley Cup in three years with a 3–0 win in New York's Madison Square Garden. It only made sense that many of the Bruin players who had just won the Cup would be considered for Team Canada for the 1972 series versus the Russians, but many might not have considered the rough-and-tumble Cashman for the list.

Sinden obviously knew what Cashman could do since he had coached the Bruins for a few years prior to the 1972 series and wanted some players who could be effective in the corners. The coach must have imagined the Russians cowering as they battled "Cash" for a loose puck as many NHL players did. He also thought that Esposito would find comfort in having at least one of his NHL wingers beside him when he faced the Soviets.

'72 Series Performance

Wayne Cashman was inserted into the Team Canada lineup after the 7–3 loss in Montreal and he had an immediate impact during the second contest in Toronto. He was determined to work over any Russian player who came near the puck when he was on the ice with his elbows and his stick. The Soviet players and coaches were upset with Cashman's rough tactics and the American referees looked the other way. He was instrumental in setting up the first goal of the game by Esposito and that seemed to give the Canadian team and the crowd in Maple Leaf Gardens a huge lift. Canada was able to slow the Russians down and that helped secure a 4–1 win. He also played in the Winnipeg game and once again assisted on a goal by Esposito — a marker that gave Canada a 3–1 lead. However, the referees were more aware of Cashman's physical approach and whistled him for two minors and a misconduct in the third period that caused him to miss half of the final frame in the 4–4 draw.

Cashman was held out of the Vancouver game and his status for any of the Moscow games might have been in question, but then something happened in Sweden that ended any thoughts of him

Now a Boston Bruin, Cashman battles with Toronto's Mike Pelyk in the late 1960s.

playing again. During the second game against the Swedes, Cashman had his tongue cut by the stick of Ulf Sterner, a Swede who had once played briefly in the NHL for the New York Rangers. It was a very bad cut and it kept Cashman out of the last four games in Moscow.

The Bruins remained a good team for a number of years and eventually named Cashman team captain when Bucyk was about to retire. Don Cherry became the Bruins' new coach and he felt Cashman had the respect of every player on the team. "Grapes" was pleased to have another native of Kingston, Ontario, in such an important role! The Bruins played in the final three more times before Cashman retired but weren't able to win the title in '74, '77, or '78. He scored 277 goals and 793 points in 1,027 games played while recording 1,041 penalty minutes — not counting the 14 he picked up against the Soviet Union. He briefly coached the Philadelphia Flyers in 1997–98 and had a winning record (32–20–9) but found he didn't like the role of head coach.

Wayne Cashman played in his first NHL game in 1964–65 when the Boston Bruins called him up (from the Oshawa Generals) for one game against the Detroit Red Wings. He was assigned to cover the Detroit great Gordie Howe! Cashman and '72 Team Canada teammate Serge Savard (who played his first NHL game in 1966–67) were the last two players from the "Original Six" era to retire. Both did so after the 1982–83 season when they were each 37 years of age.

JEAN-PAUL PARISE
Career Summary

When Jean-Paul Parise was 16 years old, he scored four goals in one game that was attended by a scout from the Boston Bruins. Parise added two assists in the same game and soon was developing his skills in the Boston system. He played just one season of major junior hockey when he was with the Niagara Falls Flyers in 1961–62 and scored eight goals in 38 games. Parise wasn't looking like an especially skilled player who was going to score much but he did become a good two-way winger and noted penalty killer. Between the ages of 21 and 25, Parise was a minor league player who couldn't get a chance at the NHL during the last years of the "Original Six," although he did get into 21 games with the Bruins where he scored two goals and added two assists.

The Bruins had many more skilled players on their team by the start of the 1967–68 season than Parise, but new jobs opened up with the six new teams added to the league. The five-foot, nine-inch, 170-pound left winger was taken by the Oakland Seals, but before he even played a game for them, Parise was traded to the Toronto Maple Leafs via a minor league trade. He spent 30 games playing for the Rochester Americans but did get into one game for the Leafs and picked up an assist. As promising as that looked, he was soon dealt to the Minnesota North Stars in a trade that saw the Leafs pick up a bunch of minor league players. It would be a terrible deal for the Toronto side but a great one for Parise who finally found a place he would call home for some time.

Parise finished 1967–68 with 11 goals in 43 games for the North Stars and seven points in 14 play-off games. The 1968–69 campaign saw him record 22 goals and 24 assists and there was no going back to the minors. By 1969–70, Parise wasn't only considered one of the best players on Minnesota but in all of the West Division of the NHL. He scored 24 times and added 48 assists for 72 points during the 76-game regular season schedule. He often played on a line with right winger Bill Goldsworthy and the pair could give opposing teams fits as they tried to contain the two North Star wingers. Parise's totals declined over the next two seasons but he

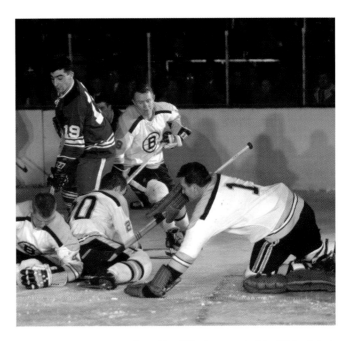

Jean-Paul Parise made his NHL debut with the Boston Bruins, but here he's a Toronto Maple Leaf and up against his old club.

was still a very effective checker and exceptional in the corners at getting pucks out to his team-mates. The 1971–72 season saw Parise score 19 times and total 37 points, which weren't great numbers compared to others, but it still got him an invitation to Team Canada for the 1972 series.

Parise's selection to the Canadian team was indeed surprising but coach Harry Sinden was very familiar with what the solid left winger could do on the ice. Sinden had seen Parise up close when the two were together in the minors in Oklahoma City and felt the North Star player could be very useful against the Russians. Sinden took his share of criticism for more than one selection to Team Canada, but he was more often correct than not.

'72 Series Performance

J.P. Parise first made an appearance in the '72 series during the game played in Toronto. Canada had been beaten in surprising fashion in the opener and Sinden wanted to set a different tone for the next game. Parise was put on the left side for centre Phil Esposito and Wayne Cashman was placed on the right side. The line was the most effective trio for Canada on the night and the crucial opening goal was scored by Esposito. The Russians weren't used to players working so hard in the corners, and Parise and Cashman made life miserable for them in that area of the ice — a big factor in the 4–1 win for Canada.

Parise had a very good game in Winnipeg, scoring just 1:54 into the game (making his father who was watching the game very proud) and adding one assist on a goal by Esposito. But when the Russians came back to tie the game 4–4, Parise was dropped from the lineup for the Vancouver game. He was back in for the first game in Moscow and snapped home a shot after a great setup by Gilbert Perreault. He played in each of the three remaining games and was a diligent worker, picking up one more assist in the seventh game. He also left a distinct impression on anyone who watched the last game.

Angered by bad calls made against Team Canada early in the eighth contest, Parise went wild after he was called for interference when a Russian player fell to the ice rather easily. Parise argued with the referee and then threatened him with his stick, which he had raised well above his head. The referee cringed as he waited for Parise to strike a blow, but the Canadian player skated away. However, it was still too late to save Parise who was ejected from the contest with more than two and a half periods still to play!

There was no defending Parise's behaviour, but the referees seemed to get the message that this winner-take-all contest was important to both teams. The rest of game saw Canada get five penalties while the Russians picked up six, so perhaps Parise had some effect in the game after all. In six games played he had four points (1G, 3A, and finished at plus one — a good series from someone many thought shouldn't have been on the team). Sinden was confident he was going to get something out of Parise over the eight-game series and the coach was rewarded for his selection by a very determined left winger.

Parise had his best NHL season in 1972–73 when he scored 27 times and added 48 assists. He would also go on to play for the New York Islanders and Cleveland Barons before ending his 890-game career with 594 points.

J.P. Parise is only one of two members of Team Canada in 1972 to have a son go on to play in the NHL. Zach Parise is currently one of the best players in the league and scored 31 goals for the New Jersey Devils in 2011–12. Pat Stapleton's son, Mike, played in 697 NHL games between 1986 and 2001 and scored 71 goals while playing for eight different teams.

BILL WHITE
Career Summary

Defenceman Bill White was one of a number of players trapped in the minors of hockey just waiting to get a chance at the big league. The native of Toronto was in the Maple Leafs system as he grew up and he played his junior hockey for the Toronto Marlboros between 1957 and 1960. The Leafs were just becoming a league power at the time and had little room for unproven players like White especially on defence, where the likes of Bobby Baun and Carl Brewer were accounting for all the young blueliners on the team. White was assigned to play in Sudbury, Ontario, and then in Rochester, New York, where he continued to develop his puck-moving skills. He caught a bit of a break when the Leafs included him in a minor league trade that saw Toronto land Kent Douglas, a 27-year-old defenceman who was also a career minor league star. White was sent to Springfield in the deal and he was one of the best defencemen in the AHL even though he had to play under the tyrannical Eddie Shore who owned the minor league club. White remained in the minors until the age of 28 when he finally got a chance in the NHL.

The Los Angeles Kings purchased the Springfield team once they joined the NHL and acquired White's rights as part of the deal. He was with the Kings in the first year of expansion and scored 11 goals and added 27 assists in 1967–68 — a very good season for a first-year player despite his slightly advanced age. He played one more season with the Kings but ended up in the middle of a contract dispute during the 1969–70 season. He was thinking of quitting, but Kings coach Hal Laycoe talked him into staying while the contract issue was being settled. The Kings were able to get White back into the fold but after 40 games were played he was sent to the Chicago Black Hawks in a six-player swap to finish out the year. The Kings received defenceman Gilles Marotte in the deal, but the Chicago side did even better because they found the perfect defensive partner for Pat Stapleton, their best blueliner.

In 1970–71, White had a terrific year (recording 25 points) and the Black Hawks made it all the way to the seventh game of the Stanley Cup finals. He registered a plus 51 rating that season (the seventh best mark in the league) and proved he belonged in the NHL for good. The six-foot, two-inch, 195-pound White was even better in 1971–72 when he was named a second-team league all-star (the first of three consecutive such nominations) while recording a 29-point season. White's game featured good positional play and excellent passes out of his own end. He also made life easier for Stapleton along the Chicago blueline by covering for his partner as needed. It only made sense that the pair of defenceman would be invited to Team Canada in 1972 and it was one of the best decisions made by the Canadian side.

'72 Series Performance

Bill White missed the first game of the series and then became a key player for the remaining seven. White was so good in the Russian series because he was able to play just like he did in the NHL. Naturally, it was very helpful that Stapleton was right beside him since the two knew each other so well, but White's main contribution was that he was so consistently good. He was one of the most focused players on Team Canada and was able to maintain his composure and discipline.

White scored just 50 goals in 604 career games in the NHL but he did manage one tally against the Russians and it was one of the biggest of the series. His only goal came in the final

Bill White, here a Los Angeles King, also played notably for the Chicago Black Hawks.
A solid defenceman, he took part in all eight Summit Series games.

game with Canada down 3–2 in the second period. White saw an opportunity and snuck in from the point to redirect a perfect pass from Rod Gilbert past Vladislav Tretiak to even the game. The final game didn't get off to a great start for White who was penalized early and the Russians capitalized (with Team Canada down two men) by scoring the first goal of the eighth game. White's goal in the second made up for getting his team down so quickly in the opening stanza.

The Soviets scored twice more after White's goal tied the game and the lanky defenceman fired a puck in the direction of one of the referees after one of those Soviet goals but, luckily, he missed the target! Canada came back to win the final game and when Paul Henderson scored the winner, White was on the ice and raced over to the group of celebrating players after he did a small jump in the air. White was very effective throughout the series by carrying the puck out of trouble and blocking many Russian shots directed at the Canadian net. By the end of the series, the Russian players didn't like many of those on Team Canada but it was clear in the end-of-game handshakes in Moscow that they all respected the way White played each contest.

White was at his best in 1972–73 when he scored nine goals and recorded a career-high 47 points. Chicago was back in the Stanley Cup finals in '73, but White missed his final chance to win a championship. He played three more seasons for the Black Hawks before his 254-point career was over as result of an injury at the age of 36.

White was traded to the Chicago Black Hawks during the 1969–70 season.

(Dennis Miles)

One thing was very noticeable about Bill White when Team Canada returned home — his jacket. White had filled the front of his Team Canada–issued sports jacket with pins and badges from every source possible for the entire month of September. It was so impressive a collection that the jacket was shown at the Hockey Hall of Fame as part of the '72 Canada-Russia series display.

PAT STAPLETON
Career Summary

One of the reasons Pat Stapleton had difficulty getting into the National Hockey League was that he was on the small side. He was a solid 180 pounds but only stood five feet, eight inches and wasn't overly physical, especially when he played defence. He was, however, very good at carrying the puck and getting it toward the opposition net. He put those skills to good use when he played forward at times and they were even more valuable when he played along the blueline. Stapleton was signed by the Chicago organization and was on the junior team in St. Catharines that won the Memorial Cup in 1960. He had 83 points (including 22 goals) in 96 junior games but the Black Hawks were too strong to fit Stapleton in at the NHL level.

Stapleton was in the minors when the Boston Bruins plucked him from Chicago and he got to play the majority of the 1961–62 season in the NHL, earning seven points in 69 games. The Bruins saw his promise but they were a very bad team at the time and were a little impatient in developing young players. He played in only 21 games (recording three assists) for the Bruins in 1962–63 before finding himself back in the minors. He spent the next three and half seasons in the minor leagues and was an excellent player for the Portland Buckaroos of the Western Hockey League (86 points in 57 games during the 1964–65 campaign). Stapleton's good play kept him in the minds of the NHL general managers and the Toronto Maple Leafs made a deal

Pat Stapleton launches himself into a rush, with Chicago Black Hawks' Denis DeJordy tending net.

with Boston that included the defenceman, but they left him unprotected for the intra-league draft in 1965. Chicago snapped up their one-time prospect but this time the Black Hawks put him on the big league roster starting with the 1965–66 campaign.

Stapleton was very impressive in his first year with Chicago, recording 34 points in 55 games and five more points in six playoff games as the Black Hawks made it to the Stanley Cup final. He was named a second-team all-star, proving that he was indeed a very talented defenceman. For the next six seasons, Stapleton was a steady performer for the Black Hawks and his assist total (31, 34, 50, 38, 44, and 38) was always at the top of the league among all blueliners. When Stapleton hit the 50-assist mark in 1968–69, it set a record for NHL defencemen, although Bobby Orr broke it the next season. He also tied an NHL record for defencemen with six assists in one game against the Detroit Red Wings in 1969.

Stapleton had to overcome a serious knee injury at the end of the 1969–70 season but he eliminated any doubts about his recovery by scoring seven goals and a total of 51 points in 1970–71. The white-haired defenceman was once again named a league all-star, but he saved his best for the '71 post-season when Chicago made it back to the finals. He recorded 17 points in 18 playoff games, but Montreal walked away with the Stanley Cup after a seven-game series. Stapleton was back on the NHL's second all-star squad after his good play in the 1971–72 season when he had 41 points in 78 games played. Stapleton's good play made him a natural for Team Canada in 1972 and his partner Bill White went along with him to play against the Russians.

'72 Series Performance

Pat Stapleton played in the last seven games of the series versus the Russians, and even though he didn't register a single point, he was very important to the success of Team Canada. He played much as he did in the NHL and his puck-lugging abilities helped get the Canadian side out of trouble time and time again. Stapleton blocked many shots especially in the games played in Moscow and he was able to deal with the fast Russian forwards by putting them into bad positions to shoot. The Russians took 227 shots on goal over the entire series, but if Stapleton hadn't been playing as well as he did there would have been many more and that likely would have meant great difficulty for Canada. On occasion Stapleton got into trouble when he gambled on the attack (he did manage eight shots on goal) but he skated hard to get back into position and foiled more than one Russian attack. He only took six minutes in penalties and was a plus six for the series.

Stapleton and White were on the ice for the final minute of the eighth game and watched as Paul Henderson scored the game winner as they stood along the Russian blueline. The pair of defencemen stayed on the ice for the final 34 seconds and White cleared the puck down the ice after the Russians made a foray into the Canadian end. The Soviets came back up the ice with 12 seconds to play and shot the puck into Team Canada's zone, but it was corralled by goalie Ken Dryden who swept it to Stapleton behind the net. Stapleton passed it to Peter Mahovlich as the clock expired.

Stapleton had another outstanding year in 1972–73, scoring a career-best 10 goals and earning another all-star selection to the second team. Chicago made it back to the Stanley Cup final once again in '73 but Montreal spoiled the celebration one more time. Stapleton then went to the World Hockey Association and made the best money of his career for the next five seasons. He finished his NHL career with 337 points in 635 games. He played in 372 WHA contests and notched 239 points to close out his career.

When Pat Stapleton passed the puck to Peter Mahovlich to close out the last game, Mahovlich looked down at the puck briefly before letting go without playing it because the game was over. Stapleton noticed the black disk just sitting there as he stood behind the net and then charged out to grab the puck after the final buzzer. For many years the puck was thought to be with Stapleton, although that was never verified. Stapleton would never comment officially about the famous puck (it was the same rubber that Henderson used to score the series-winning goal) preferring to be mysterious. In 2010 Stapleton finally admitted he had the puck, but decided he would keep it and not sell it or give it to the Hockey Hall of Fame at least until the 40th anniversary of the '72 series in 2012.

GARY BERGMAN
Career Summary

Defenceman Gary Bergman wasn't especially large at five feet, 11 inches and 188 pounds, but he was very raw-boned and wide. His father was named Gunnar (which was Bergman's middle name) and was of Swedish descent. Gunnar also played hockey as a youngster and the love of the game was passed on to the son. Bergman was up on skates around the age of three and the native of Kenora, Ontario, would eventually play his junior hockey in Winnipeg, Manitoba. Bergman was a very good defenceman for the Winnipeg Braves and helped lead the team to the Memorial Cup championship in 1959. Bergman had 24 points in 24 playoff games. Among his teammates on the Braves was another tough defenceman named Ted Green. Other future NHL players on the club included forward Bobby Leiter and goaltender Ernie Wakely.

The Montreal Canadiens owned the rights to Bergman but they won the Stanley Cup in 1959 and 1960 to close out their five consecutive championships. The Habs were very deep at that time, which meant they had no room for a young defenceman on the big league roster. As a result, Bergman was in the minors between the ages of 21 and 26 and was involved in a number of minor league trades. He was still in the Montreal organization in June 1964, but the Detroit Red Wings had watched Bergman develop his skills in the lower leagues. Detroit selected Bergman in the intra-league draft and he finally had a chance to show what he could do in the best hockey circuit.

Bergman opened the 1964–65 season with the Red Wings and would stay with Detroit until the 1973–74 season. The burly defenceman enjoyed playing a physical game, and blocking shots was one of his special skills. His offensive skills came along a little more slowly (only 11 points in 58 games during his rookie year), but by his third season Bergman hit the 30-assist mark for the first time in his career. His penalty minute total was never under 80 minutes and often well over the 100 mark (149 in 1970–71 was the highest penalty minute total in his career). Bergman gave the Red Wings a strong presence on the blueline and he became a fixture in the Motor City. He also helped the Detroit club make it to the Stanley Cup final in 1966.

Bergman settled in as a tough defender who could average about 35 points per season. The Red Wings weren't a very good

Toronto Maple Leaf Frank Mahovlich hovers as crackerjack defenceman Gary Bergman guards goalie Roy Edwards's net.

team as the decade of the 1970s began, but Bergman was the one player they could count on night in and night out. In the '70–'71 season he had 33 points for a pretty bad team and then he recorded 37 points in 1971–72 for a club that once again missed the playoffs. It came as a surprise that Bergman was selected for Team Canada in 1972, but coach Harry Sinden knew which veteran players he wanted on the club. Assistant coach John Ferguson certainly knew Bergman from butting heads with him on the ice when Montreal played Detroit over many NHL regular seasons and one playoff meeting. If other defencemen like Dallas Smith, J.C. Tremblay, and Jacques Laperriere had been able to play for Team Canada, Bergman might not have received his invite. Once he was on the team, he showed that he belonged among the best in the NHL with his play against the Russians.

'72 Series Performance

Gary Bergman was one of seven players on Team Canada to suit up for all of the eight games against the Soviet Union. He was very abrasive most of the time and made sure the Russians paid a severe price when they entered the Canadian end of the ice. At times he went a little too far with his physical edge (earning 13 penalty minutes during the series — including one five-minute major), but he also added three assists to his series record. Bergman's major contribution was being the perfect blueline partner for Brad Park. The Rangers' superstar defenceman liked to carry the puck and join the attack and that meant someone had to stay back and be mindful of the Russians coming back the other way.

It was clear Bergman was getting under the skin of some of the Russian players when he had a battle with Boris Mikhailov behind the Team Canada net late in the seventh game of the series. It ended with both players getting major penalties and the Russian player kicking Bergman more than once. The bold defenceman made all sorts of threatening gestures to more than one Russian player in the games in Moscow and he absolutely frightened one of the penalty box attendants at the Luzhniki arena! However, the penalty he took in the seventh game made it a four-on-four situation on the ice and Paul Henderson was able to use that to his advantage to score his best game-winning goal of the series. Bergman was on the ice when Yvan Cournoyer scored to tie the eighth game 5–5 in the second half of the third period.

Although Bergman didn't score a goal in any of the games, he was very nearly the hero in the final contest when he and Brad Park broke in on the Russian net with less than two minutes to play. Park set up Bergman for a great chance but Vladislav Tretiak made the save and the two Canadian defencemen had to scurry back to prevent the opposition from scoring the winning goal, so that Paul Henderson could score his dramatic winner. Bergman had given Team Canada exactly what they had hoped with his solid defensive play.

Bergman returned to the Red Wings for the 1972–73 season, but was dealt to Minnesota the following year. He missed Detroit so much he was re-acquired by the Red Wings for the 1974–75 campaign. He played one last year for the Kansas City Scouts for his final NHL season and recorded 38 points to bring his career total to 367 in 838 games played.

Gary Bergman wore sweater number 2 for most of his time as a Red Wing and he got to wear that number on Team Canada even though Brad Park wore the same number for the New York Rangers. A 35-man roster meant that many players weren't able to wear their usual NHL numbers and fans saw sweater numbers in the 30s used (for players other than goaltenders) for the first time. However, the most famous sweater of them all became Paul Henderson's number 19 on the white edition of the Team Canada uniform. The jersey, which Henderson wore while scoring the winning goal in the final game, was sold at an auction in 2011 for over $1 million.

DON AWREY
Career Summary

Defenceman Don Awrey was pretty fortunate throughout his hockey-playing days. First, he had to endure a back operation that would either cure a back condition or perhaps prevent him from ever walking again. The odds were about 50/50, but Awrey decided he had to take the risk. Everything went well and he was able to continue his hockey career. Then, by the time he was ready to be a good NHL blueliner, Awrey was on the same team as Bobby Orr, one of the greatest players ever to put on a pair of skates. Awrey was often teamed with the superstar defenceman and that helped him define his game as a physical rearguard who looked after his own end first.

Awrey came to the attention of the Boston Bruins when the Kitchener-born youngster was playing Junior B hockey. He was sent to the Niagara Falls Flyers to play Junior A in 1960–61

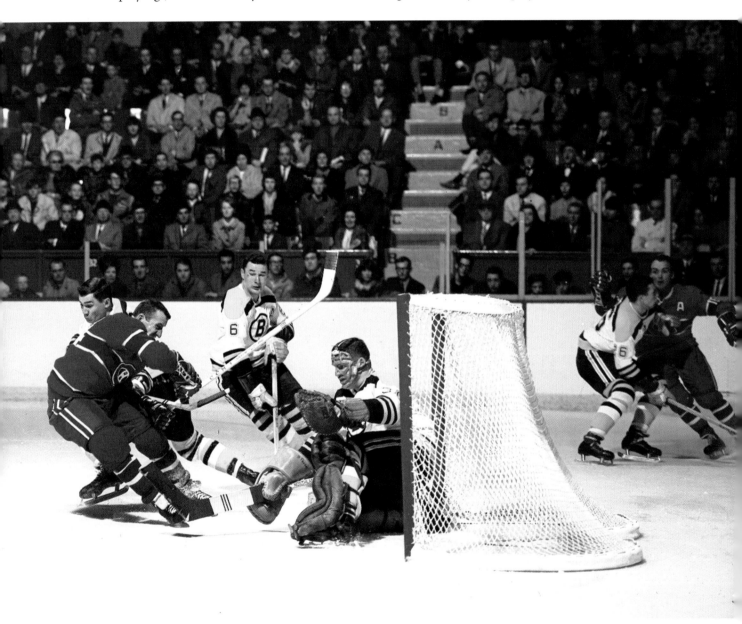

Boston Bruin Don Awrey (26) muscles Montreal's Henri Richard away from the action, while Ted Green (6) moves in to protect goalie Bernie Parent from the Habs' attack.

when he was 17 years old. The Flyers were a very good team by the 1962–63 season and many future NHL players were on the club, including Bill Goldsworthy, Gary Dornhoefer, Terry Crisp, and Ron Schock. The Flyers made it all the way to the 1963 Memorial Cup finals only to lose to the Edmonton Oil Kings. Awrey was proving to be a difficult defenceman to play against and the Bruins wanted to see what they had in the youngster.

The six-foot, 175-pound defenceman was with the Bruins for 16 games (scoring one goal) in the 1963–64 season and spent the rest of the season playing for the Minneapolis Bruins of the CPHL. He played in 47 games for Boston the next year but still spent some time in the minors with Hershey of the American Hockey League. The following year saw Awrey get a full year in the minors and he really benefited from the tutelage of Frank Mathers, the coach of the Hershey Bears. Awrey had a very good year under Mathers who had played professional hockey as a defenceman for many years. The Bruins were impressed with Awrey's progress. Bruins general manager Milt Schmidt decided to protect Awrey for the 1967 expansion draft and that allowed the rugged blueliner to start the 1967–68 season with Boston.

It was right around this time that the Bruins transformed themselves into a feared hockey club and Awrey certainly helped play a role in this change. The "Big, Bad Bruins" were born and the Boston club was in contention for the Stanley Cup for the next several years. Awrey scored very few goals (four was his best total for one season while in Boston) and his point total was usually around the 20 mark (he had 25 in 1970–71 for a very high-scoring Bruin team). Awrey's greatest strength was his work in his own end where the opposition feared going into the corners with him. He had four straight seasons in which he recorded over 100 penalty minutes. He would drop the gloves if he had to, though he wasn't considered a great fighter.

The Bruins finally won the Stanley Cup in 1970 and again in 1972. Awrey didn't score a goal in either post-season that saw Boston win it all, but he did record nine assists in 29 playoff games. He also had 67 penalty minutes over those two playoff years to keep the opposition on their toes with some tough play. He was very anxious to play for Team Canada in 1972, and when former Boston coach Harry Sinden was appointed as the bench boss for the Canadian squad, Awrey's chances of getting an invite improved greatly. He accepted the phone call telling him he was a part of the '72 team with great joy!

'72 Series Performance

Don Awrey was in the opening night lineup when the series opened up in Montreal and he is most remembered for having Valery Kharlamov skate around him before putting a shot past Ken Dryden who was in net for Team Canada. Awrey was paired with defenceman Rod Seiling and both looked as if they weren't ready to play all-out yet. It was certainly not for lack of effort but the pairing was too slow for the smaller, lightning-quick Russian forwards who were all in great shape already.

Sinden was loyal to his players and remembered what Awrey had done for him in Boston. He put the veteran blueliner back in for the fourth game in Vancouver, but that didn't work out well with Team Canada going down to a 5–3 defeat. Awrey played in the second game against the Swedes in Stockholm and he scored one of his rare goals in the 4–4 tie. However, as good as he played against the Swedes, Awrey didn't get a chance to play in any of the games in Moscow.

It is difficult to speculate how Awrey would have done on the large ice surface, but he might have been able to adjust, and the Canadian players were all rounding into shape as the series moved along. But the real strength of the Canadian team became the six defencemen they employed for the last three games in Moscow, a delicate balance the coaches couldn't tinker with in any way. Awrey did get into the game against Czechoslovakia and got on the game sheet by taking a cross-checking penalty.

Awrey was a Bruin for only one more season before he was dealt to the St. Louis Blues for a player and a second-round draft choice. He was moved to the Montreal Canadiens a year later in 1974–75 and helped them out during the regular season in 1975–76 but missed the entire playoffs when the Habs won the Stanley Cup. He also played for the Penguins, Rangers, and Rockies before closing out his 979-game career at the age of 35.

Don Awrey played in 72 games for the Montreal Canadiens during the 1975–76 season, but not in the playoffs. The '76 post-season ended with the Habs wiping out the Philadelphia Flyers in a four-game sweep in the final to take the first of four straight Stanley Cups. Despite his good performance in Montreal (12 assists and a plus 30 rating in '75–'76), Awrey's name does not appear on the Stanley Cup for that season — an injustice that should be corrected.

Awrey is also not listed on the Canadiens' '76 Stanley Cup roster in the *NHL Guide & Record Book,* but it is interesting to note that Team Canada teammate Serge Savard is now listed on the roster of Montreal's championship team of 1971 even though he didn't play a game in the playoffs. There is a notation that Savard was injured and that he had played in 37 games during the regular season.

THE
COACHES

JOHN FERGUSON
Career Summary

The Montreal Canadiens were still a very competitive team after winning their fifth straight Stanley Cup in 1960. However, they weren't of championship calibre between 1961 and 1964, which seemed like an eternity in a city used to winning titles. Nobody in Montreal would accept the Canadiens just being one of six NHL teams — they had to strive to be the best. The Habs were retooling their team with new goalies, defencemen, and forwards over a five-year period. Montreal had an abundance of skilled but small forwards and it soon became clear to management they needed a little bit of muscle if they were going to win again. Enter a five-foot, 11-inch, 190-pound 25-year-old left winger named John Ferguson who never liked to see a teammate get beaten up. Montreal's toughness issue seemed to go away pretty quickly starting with the 1963–64 season.

Ferguson was another player who was in the minors for a few seasons before he made his mark in the NHL. He played junior hockey in Saskatchewan and then played for the Fort Wayne Comets for one year before landing in Cleveland for a three-season stint in the American Hockey League. In 1962–63, Ferguson scored 38 goals in 72 games while racking up 179 penalty minutes. The Canadiens thought he was just the type of player they needed to make their smaller players more comfortable on the ice and acquired his rights from Cleveland. The hard-nosed left winger took the league by storm and, in his very first game, fought Boston tough guy Ted Green and added two goals! Ferguson scored 18 goals as a rookie and recorded 125 penalty minutes. The Habs weren't going to be pushed around anymore.

By the end of the 1964–65 season, the Canadiens were ready to recapture the Stanley Cup, and after they beat defending champion Toronto in the semi-finals, they faced the Chicago Black Hawks in the final. It went seven games with the Montreal side prevailing on home ice by a 4–0 score in the final contest. A key point in the series was Ferguson beating on Eric Nesterenko of the Black Hawks and taking some of the starch out of the Chicago club.

Ferguson was more than just a tough, intimidating player — he could score goals, notching 20 in 1966–67, the last season of the "Original Six." He led the league in penalty minutes with 177 in '66–'67, but his best year came two seasons later, in 1968–69, when he scored 29 times and had 185 minutes in penalties. He also scored the Stanley Cup–winning goal to close out the 1969 playoffs.

The final NHL season of Ferguson's career saw him win his fifth Stanley Cup after the team went through a great upheaval during the 1970–71 regular season. "Fergy," as he was known, had 10 points in 18 playoff games as the Canadiens won a surprising championship. At the age of 32, Ferguson realized it was best to retire, because many of the young tough guys would come after him now and it was going to be difficult to beat them all back. He finished his playing career with 145 goals and 1,214 penalty minutes.

He was invited to be the assistant general manager and assistant coach of Team Canada in 1972 by Harry Sinden. Ferguson always respected Sinden even though he was associated with the hated Boston Bruins. There were no coaching assistants in those days, but Sinden realized that if he was going to look after 35 players he needed some help. Ferguson had been out of hockey for one year but didn't hesitate to accept the challenge. Many of the Team Canada players were glad someone like Ferguson would be there every day because there would be less of a tendency to take things too lightly with him around. It also meant Team Canada was more likely to play with a hard, physical edge that would help and hurt the team at various times.

'72 Series Performance

John Ferguson helped Sinden pick the lineup for each game and with deciding the strategy employed in each contest. He was also very good about listening to the complaints of the players who were unhappy with their playing time or the lack of it. Vic Hadfield, Jocelyn Guevremont, and Rod Seiling were able to sound off to Ferguson and he listened to their beefs before discussing them with Sinden. Four players left the team but the others stayed, indicating that Ferguson had done a good job of controlling a volatile situation pretty well. He also helped Sinden deal with the Russian officials who weren't the least bit interested in giving Team Canada any considerations once they were in the Soviet Union.

During the games played in Moscow the assistant coach was very visible sitting at the end of the bench. Ferguson often stood up and

In his playing days with the Montreal Canadiens, John Ferguson was one of the toughest left wingers ever to lace on a pair of skates. With the Habs, he won five Stanley Cups.

offered encouragement to all the Canadian players and a few choice comments to the referees (he took one bench penalty for complaining too loudly). He urged all the players on the bench to get out on the ice with Paul Henderson when he scored late in the seventh game, fearing that the goal judge wasn't going to put on the red light at all. The celebration forced the red light to be activated, and Team Canada had the important victory assured.

The only bad moment Ferguson had was when he "suggested" to Bobby Clarke that he whack the ankle of Russian star Valery Kharlamov with his stick. It may have been thought that this action was necessary, but it was without question an unsportsmanlike move. However, it spoke to the competitive nature of John Bowie Ferguson.

Ferguson went on to become an NHL general manager with the New York Rangers (1975–76 to 1977–78) and the Winnipeg Jets (1979–80 to 1988–89). He also coached both teams briefly.

John Ferguson is the only person associated with Team Canada in 1972 to have a son go on to be an NHL general manager. John Ferguson Jr. was in charge of the Toronto Maple Leafs between 2003 and 2008. The Leafs didn't win the Stanley Cup but Ferguson had a winning percentage of .559, with 145 victories in 295 games played during his tenure in Toronto.

HARRY SINDEN
Career Summary

Harry Sinden never played in the National Hockey League and that may be attributed in part to the fact that he started in organized hockey very late. He was already 14 years old when he first started playing on a team in the Toronto area. He was noticed by a Montreal Canadiens scout a year later. After a tryout was completed, Sinden was sent to the Oshawa Generals where he played junior hockey for four seasons, starting in 1949–50. He was a good skater but not especially quick and liked to base his game around moving the puck to the open man. The Generals weren't a very good team during Sinden's time there but he did record 91 assists in 188 games as a defenceman.

He had a variety of opportunities to turn professional and chose to play for the Whitby Dunlops, a senior team, so that he could also work at General Motors at the same time. He was a very good player at this level and was named team captain in 1957. The Dunlops won the World Hockey Championships in Oslo, Norway, in 1958 with Sinden leading his team to a victory against the Russians in an outdoor rink. It was one of the greatest thrills of his hockey life since the Dunlops were representing Canada at the tournament. The victory by the Whitby club helped to restore some pride for Canada, which was no longer as dominant internationally as it once had been. Other countries like the United States were advancing, but it was the Russians who were making great leaps in world competitions with their hockey skills. Sinden played on the Canadian Olympic Team in 1960 but lost a close 2–1 contest to the Americans and had to settle for second place and a silver medal.

Sinden believed he could have made it to the NHL but never spoke up to anyone in upper management after the Boston Bruins had recruited him to play on various minor league teams in their system. Bruins general manager Lynn Patrick brought Sinden into the organization as a playing assistant coach and he was named the most valuable player in 1962–63 while he played for the Kingston Frontenacs of the EPHL. The lure of coaching had made Sinden give up his job at General Motors and eventually he was offered the Bruins' coaching position for the 1966–67 season — Bobby Orr's rookie year in the NHL. He was paid $15,000 to take the job.

Boston won just 17 games in '66–'67 but the Bruins were on their way to building a powerful team. The trade that landed them Phil Esposito got them going in the right direction and they were a Stanley Cup contender by the 1968 playoffs. Montreal beat Boston twice in the post-season before the Bruins went all the way in 1970 for their first championship in 29 years. The Bruins were a dominating team but didn't appreciate their coach, so much so that a $5,000 contract dispute ended Sinden's time behind the Boston bench. His record was 136–105–55 at the time.

Sinden missed the entire 1970–71 season, but when he was offered the position of coach of Team Canada in 1972, he simply couldn't turn the dream job down.

Playing with the Whitby Dunlops, Harry Sinden won a gold medal for Canada at the 1958 World Championships. Sinden, the captain, is seated in the first row on the far right.

'72 Series Performance

In many ways the head coaching position with Team Canada in 1972 was a thankless role. Harry Sinden knew he would have good players to choose from (even if they were only from the NHL rosters and not all of professional hockey). He had to select 35 players and then try to keep them all happy somehow. Part of the problem was that Sinden promised every player at least one game versus the Russians and that became impossible once the Soviets showed what kind of team they had. Sinden had warned his team that the Russians weren't going to be pushovers, but they weren't really listening until the end of the first game in Montreal.

Sinden's choices for the Canadian lineup were constantly questioned (even by NHL president Clarence Campbell), but he made every change thoughtfully, and once the team settled on six defencemen, the whole club started to play better with each contest. He didn't like having to deal with unhappy players who weren't going to get into the games versus the Russians, but he was grateful to all those who stayed with the team until the very end.

At times Sinden lost his cool behind the bench (he tossed a stool or small bench on the ice in Moscow), and that may have affected how his team played on the ice — too angry and undisciplined at moments. Certainly he had a right to be upset with the officiating throughout the series (it wasn't close to NHL calibre), but if anyone knew international refereeing left a great deal to be desired, it was the Canadian head coach.

Sinden's finest moment may have come after the first game when he was preparing for the next contest in Toronto, a mere 48 hours later. The Canadian team was in no better physical condition just two nights later, but Sinden and his assistant John Ferguson made the right personnel choices and altered Team Canada's style of play to slow the Russians down rather than trying to beat them with many offensive-minded players (as they had in Montreal). He was also quick to recognize that the series wasn't going to be 8–0 in Canada's favour and adjusted his mindset to reflect that reality. After it was over and Canada had just edged out the Russians, all Sinden could say was "it was never in doubt."

The Boston Bruins came to their senses and hired Sinden back — this time as their general manager. He kept the job from 1972 until 2000. The Bruins never won the Stanley Cup with Sinden as the general manager but they made it to the final five times.

When the Boston Bruins won the Stanley Cup in 2011, Harry Sinden was listed as a senior adviser to the team owner Jeremy M. Jacobs. Sinden's name is listed on the Cup roster in the *NHL Guide & Record Book* and was etched into the silver trophy for the second time.

A FINAL WORD ON THE TITANS OF '72

In the summer and fall of 2012, Team Canada players will gather to celebrate the 40th anniversary of the 1972 Canada-Russia Series. A lot has changed in the past 40 years, but the players share a special bond that has been with them since they first got together in Maple Leaf Gardens on a hot afternoon in August 1972. They shared the highs and lows of the incredible eight-game Summit Series and have always thought of themselves in some way as soldiers who went to war. Their lives have been intertwined ever since the series ended in what was a great triumph for them and Canada. The Soviet Union that existed in 1972 is no more and Canada is also a different nation, but that doesn't take away from the great memories of one stupendous September four decades ago.

One of the projected outcomes of the '72 series was that other international competitions would emerge. That hope was fulfilled and Canada enjoyed more great moments: Darryl Sittler scoring in overtime to win the first ever Canada Cup; Mario Lemieux shooting the winner against the Russians to clinch the 1987 Canada Cup; Sidney Crosby firing home the overtime winner to give Canada the gold medal at the 2010 Winter Olympic Games in Vancouver; and many others. These great moments might never have happened had it not been for the thrills and excitement Team Canada first created in 1972. It was there that we learned this type of competition could be an exciting brand of hockey — maybe the best.

The game of hockey was never the same after the '72 series. Canada had to accept that the rest of the world was going to improve the game we called our own. So many more countries play the sport at a much higher level than ever before and that has allowed the National Hockey League to expand to 30 teams. It has also made international tournaments much more interesting with at least five to six nations having a legitimate chance to win any time hockey nations gather. Canada wins more than its share of these worldwide competitions, but the shock of another nation beating a talented Canadian team has worn off almost completely. Players from Russia and surrounding states are still very formidable opponents but the main rival for the throne of the best hockey nation in 2012 appears to be coming from a source much closer to home — the United States.

As much as Canadians have accepted change, they still have a special place reserved in the history books for the 1972 series. Canada and Russia have played many games since 1972, but it has never been quite the same. On occasion there has been talk of another series but it never amounts to anything. Those eight games played over 28 days in September will never be repeated and that is why names like Esposito, Henderson, Ellis, Dryden, Park, Cournoyer, Savard, Stapleton, and White, to name a few, will always be a part of a team that lives on in our hearts. It is fortunate that the tapes of the 1972 series have been saved and are available to everyone who wants to relive a special part of Canada's sporting history. Enjoying the games over again for those who were around in 1972 will bring a smile to their faces and rekindle a special memory of where they were on September 28, 1972. Those viewing the games for the very first time will learn why the 1972 Team Canada was named the "Team of the Century" and why the Titans of '72 were a special group of players.

Dejection for goaltender Vladislav Tretiak; jubilation for Team Canada after Paul Henderson's dramatic game-winning goal in Game 7. [Frank Lennon/GetStock.com]

GAME SUMMARIES

Game 1: Saturday, September 2, 1972, Montreal
RUSSIANS STUN ALL OF CANADA WITH 7–3 WIN IN SERIES OPENER

After all the pomp and circumstance to open this historic series was over, Team Canada roared out of the starting blocks and jumped out to a quick 1–0 lead on a goal by Phil Esposito just 30 seconds into the game. Paul Henderson scored on a face-off six minutes later to make it 2–0 and everyone was thinking, "Can it really be this easy?" The short answer to that question was a resounding no. Before the first period was over the Russians had tied the score 2–2 and the once-tense but confident crowd at the Montreal Forum was now very nervous and unsure.

The second period was a very difficult one for Team Canada as they gave up the only two goals of the middle frame. Russian winger Valery Kharlamov was brilliant and potted both goals for the Soviets. It is interesting to note that the teams each took 10 shots on goal, but it looked as if Team Canada was having difficulty keeping up on what was a very warm evening in the Montreal Forum. The Russians were faster and Team Canada seemed unable to slow them down.

Bobby Clarke gave Canada hope in the first half of the third period and suddenly the Canadian team had some life down just one at 4–3. They pressed into the Russian end and peppered Vladislav Tretiak in the Russian net, but he stood firm as he had all night long. The Russians counterattacked and before anyone knew what happened, the Soviets had put three more goals (Mikhailov, Zimin, and Yakushev) past Ken Dryden. The Canadian goalie was sprawled on the ice most of the night unable to make any heart-stopping saves, but also not getting much help from the Team Canada defence.

Shocked at the turn of events, the Canadian team forgot to line up for the post-game hand-shakes, although Dryden and forward Red Berenson acknowledged the Russians with a wave. Team Canada said they were unaware of the post-game requirement, but they did try to return to the ice only to find the Russians had already left.

Team Canada coach Harry Sinden was left to contemplate what had just happened to his team of all-stars and knew he had to make some changes for the next game in Toronto. The Canadian side didn't look like a team while the Russians seemed like a well-oiled machine by comparison. The overall tempo of the game had been far too fast for Canada and they would have to devise a game plan where they could slow the Soviets down and reduce the speed advantage they clearly possessed in the opener. Canada had to take some comfort in the fact that it was a one-goal game with less than seven minutes to go, but had to be concerned they faded so badly that the Russians won the game going away.

All Canadians were surprised and upset with the result of the game they had waited so long to see. How the team and fans were going to react for the next game just two days later was the big question.

Game 2: Monday, September 4, 1972, at Toronto
ESPOSITO BROTHERS LEAD TEAM CANADA TO VICTORY

Changes were the order of the day for the Team Canada roster and coach Harry Sinden made all the right moves on this night. Tony Esposito was in net for Canada and he was splendid the entire game. Phil Esposito showed great heart and desire up front and scored the all-important opening goal for Canada in the second period.

The crowd at Maple Leaf Gardens was clearly behind Team Canada and that seemed to give the team a significant boost of energy. The tension was heightened when Team Canada was penalized twice in the opening period but they managed to kill off both minors. Wayne Cashman and Jean-Paul Parise were very effective at taking the body against the Soviets and centre Stan Mikita played like the feisty player he was in the NHL. Canada was helped greatly by additions to the blueline that included Pat Stapleton, Bill White, and Serge Savard. All three of these defenders could move the puck out of the Canadian end.

The Russians didn't like the way the Canadians were playing in this game and were upset with how the two American referees (Steve Dowling and Frank Larsen) called this game. They took three minors in the second period and were called for a 10-minute misconduct, which was given to the sublimely talented Kharlamov. There would have been another penalty assessed at the 7:14 mark of the middle frame, but Esposito scored from right in front of the Russian goal to make it 1–0 for Team Canada while the referee still had his arm raised. That goal seemed to give the Canadian side more confidence that they could win this contest, but it was still a one-goal game going into the third.

Brad Park sprung Yvan Cournoyer with a long pass just 1:19 into the final frame and the "Roadrunner" made no mistake when he went around the Russian defence before snapping a shot past Tretiak. The Russians got one back on a goal by Yakushev when he rapped home a rebound past Tony Esposito, the only mistake on the night by the Canadian netminder. Then a penalty to Stapleton gave the Soviets a chance to tie the game.

However, Phil Esposito knocked the puck off the boards in the Canadian end and the puck went straight to Peter Mahovlich who scored one of the classic goals in hockey history. He got past a defenceman and then deked Tretiak before backhanding the puck into the net. Canada was up 3–1. The effort and reaction to the Mahovlich goal deflated the Russians and gave Team Canada all they needed to secure the win. A late goal by Frank Mahovlich made it a 4–1 final and the Russian only had 21 shots on goal for the entire game.

Everyone associated with Team Canada was ecstatic about winning the Toronto game but it was a close, tight contest throughout. The Canadians had succeeded in slowing the Soviets down, and although some of the hits and stick work were indeed questionable, Team Canada had done what was necessary to get a victory in this game — a must-win even this early in the series. As much as Team Canada enjoyed the win at Maple Leaf Gardens, nobody was quite sure what the next game in Winnipeg would bring.

Game 3: Wednesday, September 6, 1972, at Winnipeg
CANADA CANNOT HOLD LEAD AND SETTLE FOR A 4–4 DRAW

Building off their good game in Toronto, the Canadian team got off to a good start at the Winnipeg Arena and scored just 1:54 into the game. Jean-Paul Parise knocked in a loose puck in front of Tretiak to make it 1–0. But this turn of events didn't seem to faze the Russians one bit. Less than two minutes later the Soviets jumped on a giveaway by Frank Mahovlich and Vladimir Petrov capitalized by drilling a shot past Tony Esposito to even the score. But late in the opening frame, Cournoyer and Jean Ratelle combined on a pretty play to give Canada a 2–1 lead at the end of the first period. Ratelle scored the go-ahead goal and made his re-insertion into the Team Canada lineup look like a smart move by the coaches. The sequence that led to Ratelle's goal was started by Paul Henderson who threw a clean check at the Russian player carrying the puck. Gary Bergman picked up the loose disk and gave it to Cournoyer starting the attack into the Soviet end.

Phil Esposito scored before five minutes had passed in the second period after shooting one in from his now-customary spot in the slot. However, Kharlamov got the Russians right back into the game when he broke in alone, protecting the puck beautifully before pulling Esposito out of the goal and depositing a shot in the empty net at the 12:56 mark of the second. Less than a minute later the speedy Paul Henderson broke in over the Soviet blueline and slapped a perfectly placed shot into the far side of the net past a startled Tretiak. The Henderson goal gave Canada another two-goal lead but Yuri Lebedev and Alexander Bodunov scored two goals in less than four minutes to even the game 4–4 before the end of the second period.

The third period saw no scoring but the most significant moment came when Henderson was robbed point blank by Tretiak. The Canadian winger was so sure his shot was going to beat Tretiak that he had his arms raised ready to celebrate. Instead, Henderson had to end his celebration very abruptly and he went over to say a word or two to Tretiak. It is unknown what Henderson said, but it looked as if it was a friendly exchange, although the Soviet goalie wasn't able to speak or understand English. The Russians had the lone power play of the final period and Wayne Cashman was given a 10-minute misconduct when he argued his minor penalty call too strongly.

Team Canada saw another side of the Soviet Union they may not have been prepared for — the Russian ability to mount a comeback when they were down. They came back twice from two-goal deficits and showed no sign of wilting under Team Canada's physical style. The

Russians only took 25 shots on goal but made the most of their drives with four tallies while the Canadian team had to fire 38 at Tretiak to achieve the same result. The Soviets were also not afraid to insert youngsters into the lineup and added three 21-year-olds (Anisin, Lebedev, and Bodunov) to the roster for this game

Seeing his team unable to hold the lead made coach Sinden re-examine his roster for the fourth game in Vancouver. Team Canada needed another win to close off the Canadian portion of the series and to gain the lead before the scene shifted to Moscow. It would prove to be an impossible task.

Game 4: Friday, September 8, 1972, at Vancouver
BOOS UPSET TEAM CANADA DURING 5–3 LOSS TO SOVIETS

To put it very directly nothing went right for Team Canada in the fourth game of the '72 series. Almost none of the lineup changes implemented by Sinden and Ferguson worked, and the Russians were quick to pounce on a very shaky opponent. Canada was missing two key defencemen in this contest — Serge Savard and Guy Lapointe of the Montreal Canadiens — but it is very doubtful their presence could have saved the Canadian club on this night.

It all got off to a horrible start when winger Bill Goldsworthy took two first-period penalties — both of the very bad and unnecessary variety — and the Russians scored on both power-play opportunities. Boris Mikhailov notched both Soviet goals and the Canadian team never recovered from the two-goal deficit. Gilbert Perreault, playing in his first game for Canada, scored a beauty of a goal by taking the puck end-to-end before beating Tretiak to make it 2–1 early in the second but that was the only Canadian highlight of the night. The Russians scored twice more in the middle frame to make it a 4–1 game going into the third period. The Vancouver crowd showed no patience with Team Canada and were especially hard on the home team when they took bad penalties. There was no sense of support for Team Canada and it only got worse in the third period.

Goldsworthy redeemed himself a little when he put in a rebound at the 6:54 mark of the third to get Canada within two. However, any thoughts of a comeback were quickly doused when Shadrin scored for Russia to make it 5–2. A very late goal by Dennis Hull at 19:38 made it a little more respectable but Team Canada was roundly booed when the game was over. None of the Canadian players reacted well to the booing. They were very upset by the reaction of the Vancouver fans. Many felt that playing for your country meant something special — like being in the nation's army — and therefore nobody would ever boo someone wearing a Canadian uniform.

Phil Esposito took matters into his own hands during a post-game television interview and let loose on Canadian fans who were booing or criticizing the team. He didn't use any bad language nor was he especially eloquent but Esposito spoke from the heart and clearly made the point that he didn't think it was fair that Team Canada should be booed on home ice. He did use the word *disappointed* a few times and said many of the Team Canada players were down about how they were being treated. It was also evident he was speaking for the whole team.

"Espo" had taken the leadership reins and it paid dividends almost as soon as he left the ice because he already had a phone call of support from a Canadian fan in Newfoundland. It was an important turn of events for Team Canada, which now had to wait until September 22 to get at the Soviets in Moscow.

Game 5: Friday, September 22, 1972, at Moscow
SOVIETS EXPLODE WITH FIVE THIRD-PERIOD GOALS TO WIN 5–4

Team Canada spent the 14 days between games with the Soviets by playing two games in Stockholm against the Swedish national team. Canada won the first game 4–1 and tied the second 4–4, but their rough play got the whole team in trouble with those who attended the games. One player, Wayne Cashman, was injured in one of the melees that ensued against the Swedes and was gone for the rest of the Soviet series. Team Canada finally got all the players on the roster some playing time (except for Bobby Orr) and they got an opportunity to adjust to the wider (by about 12 to 15 feet) international rinks. Despite problems on and off the ice in Sweden, the games were a bonding experience designed to bring Team Canada together.

Team Canada no longer appeared to be a group of strangers when they hit the ice in Moscow for the fifth game of the series. They took the game to the Russians and were rewarded with a 3–0 lead going into the third period. Jean-Paul Parise snapped home a Gilbert Perreault pass to open the scoring at the 15:30 mark of the first period. Bobby Clarke with his second of the series scored 2:36 into the second period, followed by another marker by Paul Henderson at 11:36 of the middle frame. Henderson crashed into the boards in the second and was knocked out for a few minutes. He came around in the dressing room and insisted he play despite the team doctor telling him he had a concussion. He appealed to Sinden who gave Henderson the go-ahead.

If Henderson was feeling better, the rest of the team fell asleep in the third period and it was the worst 20 minutes of the entire series for the Canadian squad. Yuri Blinov scored 3:34 into the final frame to break Tony Esposito's shutout bid, but Henderson took a long pass from Clarke and went in alone to slap a drive past Tretiak. That goal made it 4–1 for Canada, but there were still 15 minutes to play.

The unthinkable started happening when Anisin scored at the 9:05 mark. That goal was quickly followed up with goals from Shadrin at 9:13 and Gusev at 11:41. The score was now tied 4–4 and the Canadian team was looking bad in all areas of the ice. Jean Ratelle missed a great chance to give Canada the lead once again, but his shot hit the post behind Tretiak. With just under six minutes to play, Clarke and Rod Seiling combined to lose the puck and Victor Vikulov beat Esposito to give the Russians a 5–4 lead. Alexander Yakushev was given a penalty at 15:48 of the final frame but Canada couldn't score with the power-play chance.

The Russians had once again shown the heart needed to come back, while Team Canada looked very weak in its effort to protect a three-goal lead. The Soviets took 33 shots on goal while Canada had 37 in a rather wide-open affair where both teams took turns being sloppy. However, the end result was that the Russians needed a win or a tie in the remaining games to keep Canada from winning the series. To their credit, the Team Canada players didn't waver in their belief that they could come back and win the series.

Game 6: Sunday, September 24, 1972, at Moscow
CANADA SCORES THREE QUICK GOALS TO WIN 3–2

With no room for error, Team Canada played their best 60 minutes of the series since the Toronto game to eke out a 3–2 victory. Cheered on by close to 3,000 Canadian fans in attendance in Moscow, the Canadian team scored three goals in the second period to gain the margin of victory they so desperately needed. The Russians had opened the scoring in the second period when Liapkin beat Ken Dryden at the 1:12 mark of the middle frame. But then Team Canada went to work in lightning fashion.

The comeback began with the little-used Dennis Hull slapping one past Tretiak at the 5:13 mark of the second. That marker was followed up by Yvan Cournoyer (after taking a nice pass from Red Berenson) at 5:21. Paul Henderson let a drive go from just inside the Russian blueline that somehow got by Tretiak at 5:36 to give Canada a 3–1 lead. Big Alexander Yakushev scored at 17:11 of the second to bring the Soviets within one but the Canadians checked very well in the third period and hung on to win. For one of the very few times in the series, the Russian took more shots on goal (29 to 22) than Team Canada, but the revamped Canadian defence was very strong in this game.

Two outcomes were very clear from this contest. The first was the good play of goalie Ken Dryden. He stopped the opening shot taken by the Soviets and that seemed to give him some confidence. Dryden had played in many important playoff games and had already won a Stanley Cup but the pressure he was under in this game must have at least rivalled what he felt during his finest NHL performances. The six-foot, four-inch Dryden made many key stops during this game and held the Soviets off the scoreboard. His best save may have actually been a goal (it looked as if the puck had hit the mesh that hung down behind Dryden on a point-blank scoring attempt by Kharlamov with about half the net to shoot at) when Canada was down two men and clinging to a 3–2 lead. Dryden somehow managed to snare the puck with his glove and neither referee saw the puck enter the net, but the Russians did protest briefly. Luckily for Team Canada there were no goal reviews available with video replays. Dryden also held the Russians off during a late-game power play when Ron Ellis was called on a highly questionable penalty call at 17:39 of the final frame.

The other noticeable development was that for the very first time the Russians seemed to let up. They didn't match the desperation of Team Canada and couldn't seem to find the energy to make another comeback. The Soviet coaches might have tweaked their lineup too much for this game, weakening their defence. The Russians might have been the ones who were overconfident in this game and it showed.

Soviet sniper Valery Kharlamov was whacked hard on the ankle by Bobby Clarke and he would never be effective again in the series (the slick Russian missed the seventh game altogether). It wasn't Canada's finest moment but the entire team was under excruciating pressure to win and some actions were reflective of their need for victory no matter the cost.

Canada was now back in the series and feeling a whole lot better with their first victory since they had won in Toronto! It was now a matter of staying focused on the end result and winning two more games.

Game 7: Tuesday, September 26, 1972, at Moscow
PAUL HENDERSON SCORES LATE GOAL TO EVEN SERIES

It was only fitting that a great goal ended one of the best hockey games ever played. Team Canada winger Paul Henderson got past two Russian defencemen before putting a high shot over Vladislav Tretiak's shoulder while sliding on the ice for the game winner. The tremendous effort by the Toronto Maple Leaf star with just 2:06 to play gave the Canadian side a 4–3 win and kept the hopes of a Team Canada series win alive. A loss to the Soviets would have meant the Russians would have won the series and the eighth game would have been rendered meaningless.

Phil Esposito got Canada off to a good start in this game when he scored at the 4:09 mark of the opening period. However, the Soviet Union scored twice to take a 2–1 lead on goals by Yakushev (on a beautiful, well-placed slap shot that handcuffed goalie Tony Esposito) and Petrov. Once again, Phil Esposito drew Canada even with the assists going to Jean-Paul Parise and Serge Savard. There was no scoring in the second period but that set up a very dramatic final frame.

Rod Gilbert scored on a quick backhand shot to give Canada a 3–2 lead just 2:13 into the last period. However, Canada couldn't stand the prosperity and let Yakushev tie the game three minutes later. The tense contest remained tied 3–3 late in the contest when a nasty struggle broke out between Gary Bergman of Canada and Boris Mikhailov of the Soviet Union. There was kicking involved and Yvan Cournoyer came to the aid of his teammate with some rough play against the feisty Russian. The result was that both Bergman and Mikhailov were given major penalties (although neither was ejected) at 16:26 of the third. That meant the last few minutes of the contest were going to feature four-on-four play exclusively.

Bobby Clarke won a face-off in the Team Canada end and Guy Lapointe made sure the puck got to defensive partner Serge Savard. The big Canadian defenceman swept around the boards with the puck on his stick before getting it to Henderson just past the Canadian blueline. At one point Henderson had all four Russians within a few feet of him, but the two backchecking forwards peeled away. He approached the two Soviet defencemen and tried to make an outside move but one defender went for a bodycheck and only got a piece of Henderson. The other Russian defenceman went for the puck but missed it. Suddenly Henderson was in the clear but sliding along the ice with the puck out in front of him. He saw Tretiak go down and managed to snap a shot into the top corner of the Russian net.

The Canadian team came off the bench to mob Henderson who had just scored a miracle goal with time running out. It was an incredible individual effort by Henderson but Savard's contribution to the game winner should also be remembered. Canada killed off the remaining couple of minutes for a 4–3 win and now had a chance to win the series on Thursday night in Moscow. The series was all tied up at 3–3–1 with one game to go, a situation no one would have predicted at the start of the series!

Game 8: Thursday, September 28, 1972, at Moscow
TEAM CANADA SCORES WITH 34 SECONDS TO PLAY TO TAKE SERIES

In a wildly improbable finish to a game that had just about everything, Team Canada found a way to score a last-minute goal to win 6–5 and take the series by a 4-3-1 margin. Once again it was Paul Henderson who scored the winning goal (the third consecutive game he had done so), this time with just 34 seconds to play.

The eighth game almost never happened, because the two sides couldn't agree on who should referee it. They reached a compromise in the middle of the afternoon but nobody was very happy. Team Canada was especially unhappy early in the game when they took three of the four penalties called early on. Jean-Paul Parise was called for interference and was wildly upset about the call. He nearly attacked referee Josef Kompalla with his stick and earned a game misconduct for losing his temper.

Alexander Yakushev scored early at the 3:34 mark while two Team Canada players were in the penalty box. Phil Esposito tied the game on a Team Canada power play but the Russians scored to make it 2–1 while Yvan Cournoyer was off serving a penalty. Brad Park finished off a nice rush with Jean Ratelle to even the game at 2–2 but the situation got worse for the Canadians in the second period.

Shadrin took advantage of a good bounce off the mesh behind the net to score just 21 seconds into the second period. Goaltender Ken Dryden had no chance to make the save. Team Canada defenceman Bill White jumped into the attack to make it 3–3 halfway through the second, but Yakushev scored to make it 4–3 for the Soviets. Another Canadian penalty to Pat Stapleton allowed the Russians to score a goal by Vasiliev. Canada had battled hard, but the team was now down 5–3 with one period to play. Surprisingly the spirits in the Team Canada dressing room were still high and they decided to let it all hang out for one more period and see what would happen.

It all came together for Team Canada when Esposito, who was great in all areas of the ice for the entire game, scored at the 2:27 mark of the final period. Down only by one the Canadian side pressed for the equalizer and got it when Esposito and Cournoyer crashed the Russian goal. After a wild scramble in front of the net, Cournoyer backhanded a shot in to tie the game 5–5 at the 12:56 mark of the third.

The Soviets were reeling at this point, unable to match the desire of the Canadian team for a victory. The Soviets seemed content to let the clock run out and leave the game tied at 5–5. With under a minute to go, Henderson began hollering at Peter Mahovlich to get to the bench for a change. As Henderson jumped onto the ice, the puck was trapped by Cournoyer along the far boards. He tried to hit Henderson with a pass but number 19 fell and slid into the boards. The puck lay tantalizingly in the face-off circle and the first person to get there was Esposito.

The big centre whacked the puck on goal but it was stopped. Henderson was now in front of the net for the rebound, which Tretiak also stopped but without controlling or trapping the puck. It came back out to Henderson who made no mistake this time, and a wild celebration ensued as Canada took the lead for good. An incredible comeback for Team Canada was now complete and the series-ending goal by Henderson would be forever remembered as the greatest moment in Canadian sports history.

Although this game might not have been a technical masterpiece, it was a contest that featured high drama, great suspense, and tremendous emotion. This game between two great hockey nations would ultimately hold a high place in the history of hockey well beyond September 1972.

BIBLIOGRAPHY

Books

Cohen, Ross, John Halligan, and Adam Raider. *100 Ranger Greats.* Toronto: John Wiley & Sons, 2009.

Coleman, Jim. *Hockey Is Our Game.* Toronto: Key Porter Books, 1987.

Conacher, Brian. *As the Puck Turns.* Toronto: John Wiley & Sons, 2007.

Dryden, Ken. *Face-Off at the Summit.* Toronto: Little, Brown Canada, 1972.

Ellis, Ron, and Kevin Shea. *Over the Boards: The Ron Ellis Story.* Bolton, ON: Fenn Publishing, 2002.

Esposito, Phil. *Thunder and Lightning.* Toronto: McClelland & Stewart, 2003.

Ferguson, John. *Thunder and Lightning.* Toronto: Prentice-Hall, 1989.

Fischler, Stan. *Bobby Orr and the Big, Bad, Bruins.* New York: Dodd, Mead, 1969.

Fisher, Dave. *Hockey: The New Champions.* New York: Platt & Munk, 1973.

Hadfield, Vic. *Vic Hadfield's Diary.* New York: Doubleday, 1974.

Henderson, Paul. *Shooting for Glory.* Toronto: Stoddart, 1991.

Hewitt, Foster. *Hockey Night in Canada.* Toronto: Ryerson Press, 1961.

Hockey Canada. *1972 CANADA/U.S.S.R. Series.* Montreal: NSP Limited, 1972.

Hodge, Charlie. *Golly Gee It's Me! The Howie Meeker Story.* Toronto: Stoddart, 1996.

Hollander, Zander. *The Complete Handbook of Pro Hockey — 1972 Edition.* New York: Lancer Books, 1972.

Lapp, Richard, and Alec Macaulay. *The Memorial Cup.* Madeira Park, BC: Harbour Publishing, 1998.

Leonetti, Mike. *The Game We Knew: Hockey in the Seventies.* Vancouver: Raincoast, 1999.

____. *Defining Moments.* Markham, ON: Red Deer Press, 2011.

Mahovlich, Ted. *The Big M.* Toronto: HarperCollins Canada, 2000.

____. *The Marcel Dionne Story.* Toronto: HarperCollins Canada, 2004.

Martin, Lawrence. *The Red Machine.* Toronto: Doubleday Canada, 1990.

McFarlane, John. *Twenty-Seven Days in September.* Toronto: Hockey Canada Publications, 1973.

Morrison, Scott. *The Days Canada Stood Still.* Toronto: McGraw-Hill Ryerson, 1989.

Park, Brad. *Play the Man.* New York: Warner Books, 1971.

Proudfoot, Jim. *Pro Hockey 1970–71.* Toronto: Simon & Schuster, 1970.

Sinden, Harry. *Hockey Showdown.* Toronto: Doubleday Canada, 1972.

Terroux, Gilles, and Denis Brodeur. *Face-Off of the Century.* Toronto: Collier-Macmillan of Canada, 1972.

Tretiak, Vladislav. *Tretiak: The Legend.* Edmonton: Plains Publishing, 1987.

Young, Scott. *War on Ice: Canada in International Hockey.* Toronto: McClelland & Stewart, 1976.

Magazines

Action Sports 1971–72 Hockey Yearbook
Hockey Digest
Hockey Illustrated
Hockey Pictorial
Hockey World
Sports Illustrated

Record Books

NHL Guide and Record Book
Total NHL

Websites

"1972 Summit Series.com: A September to Remember." *www.1972summitseries.com* (accessed June 10, 2012).
"Hockey-Reference.com | Hockey Statistics and History." *http://Hockey-reference.com* (accessed June 10, 2012).
"Hockey Hall of Fame Homepage." *www.hhof.com* (accessed June 10, 2012).
"The Internet Hockey Database — Hockey Statistics, Data, Logos, and Trading Cards." *www. hockeydb.com* (accessed June 10, 2012).
"NHL.com — The National Hockey League." *www.nhl.com* (accessed June 10, 2012).
"YouTube — Broadcast Yourself." *www.youtube.com* (accessed June 10, 2012).

Newspapers

Articles from the Canadian Press from September and October 1972
Toronto Star
Globe and Mail

Television

Original broadcasts of all eight games on CBC or CTV

Radio

Original broadcast of Game 8 from Moscow on CBC Radio

OTHER GREAT HOCKEY BOOKS

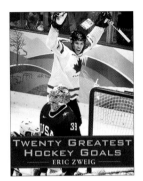

TWENTY GREATEST HOCKEY GOALS
by Eric Zweig
978-1554887897
$24.99

Every hockey fan remembers certain goals scored that stand out from all others. But if one had to name just 20 as the greatest ever accomplished, what would they be? Author Eric Zweig does just that in *Twenty Greatest Hockey Goals*. Here you'll find everything from Paul Henderson's third game-winning goal in the 1972 Canada-Soviet Summit Series to Sidney Crosby's "golden goal" in the 2010 Vancouver Winter Olympics, not to mention Mike Eruzione's upset "Miracle on Ice" winner for the United States against the Soviets at Lake Placid in 1980 and Wayne Gretzky's 77th goal in 1982 to beat Phil Esposito's single-season scoring record.

HOPE AND HEARTBREAK IN TORONTO
Life as a Maple Leafs Fan
by Peter Robinson
978-1459706835
$19.99

What does it mean to be a fan of the Toronto Maple Leafs? Ultimately, it requires an ability to endure inevitable disappointment while still taking a huge leap of faith on a yearly basis. Author Peter Robinson has attended some 125 games over the past six seasons, but has yet to be rewarded for his dedication by any substantial wins from the Leafs. Why do he and all his fellow fans keep coming back? Why does a team that hasn't won the Stanley Cup since 1967, or even been in the final, have such a hold on its fans? Robinson probes deeply into the collective mind of Toronto hockey fans and into the nature of the very sport itself to answer these intriguing questions.

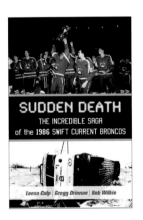

SUDDEN DEATH
The Incredible Saga of the 1986 Swift Current Broncos
by Leesa Culp, Gregg Drinnan, and Bob Wilkie
978-1459705449
$25.99

On December 30, 1986, the Swift Current Broncos set out for Regina to play the Pats. A few kilometres east of Swift Current their bus left the highway and four players died in the crash. This tragedy shook the world of hockey to its core. However, more dramatic events were to unfold. Authors Leesa Culp, Gregg Drinnan and Bob Wilkie recount the remarkable aftermath of that fateful day: the Broncos' remarkable Memorial Cup win in 1989 and then the shocking charges of sexual assault put forth by Sheldon Kennedy and others against Graham James, the Broncos' once-respected coach.

DUNDURN
www.dundurn.com

Visit us at
Dundurn.com
Definingcanada.ca
@dundurnpress
Facebook.com/dundurnpress